This Gladdening Light

An Ecology of Fatherhood and Faith

Christopher Martin

MERCER UNIVERSITY PRESS | *Macon, Georgia*

2017

MUP/ P544

© 2017 by Mercer University Press
Published by Mercer University Press
1501 Mercer University Drive
Macon, Georgia 31207

9 8 7 6 5 4 3 2 1

Books published by Mercer University Press are printed on acid-free paper that meets the requirements of the American National Standard for Information Sciences—Permanence of Paper for Printed Library Materials.

ISBN   978-0-88146-615-7
Cataloging-in-Publication Data is available from the Library of Congress

for Deana, Cannon, and Opal,
my lights

THE WILL D. CAMPBELL AWARD WINNERS

2010 Kathy Bradley, *Breathing and Walking Around*
(Published 2012)

2011 No Award Given

2012 Joseph Bathanti, *Half of What I Say Is Meaningless*
(Published 2014)

2013 No Award Given

2014 Bill Merritt, *Crackers*
(Published 2016)

2015 Chris Martin, *This Gladdening Light*
(Published 2017)

Contents

...this life was the glimmering of people,
and this glimmering shone in a void,
and the void itself couldn't hold on anymore.
                    —Gospel of John

Be on your guard so that no one deceives you by saying
'Look over here!' or 'Look over there!' For a child
who remembers how to be human exists within you.
Follow it: Those who search for it will find it.
                    —Gospel of Mary

God's in a tree and in every people.
                    —Opal, my daughter, at age three

Preface

God Sits Drawing Whales

Leviathan leaves a shining path in its wake.

—Job 41:32

I am drafting this preface on a chilly April morning, 2016. My children—ages six and four—are sitting at a small table in the kitchen, drawing pictures of whales. Every so often they'll argue about whose whale is better. My daughter, the younger of the two, goads my son by telling him he doesn't even know how to draw a whale. She says she's drawing a sperm whale, and gets up to show it to me as I sit here writing.

She's used colored pencils and her page bursts with light, as though her sperm whale were swimming in a rainbow, with another rainbow fuming from its blowhole. She's also dotted her page with little black blobs. When I ask what they are, she tells me they're chocolate chips. I tell her that her picture is beautiful.

My son, using crayons, is drawing a blue whale and a narwhal, the former situated above the latter, on the same wide piece of white construction paper, like a plate one might see in a field guide to sea mammals—grays, browns, subtle blues. He's written the names of the creatures beneath each one.

We are all in this moment following art that is inherently eco-logical. *Ecology*, as I understand it, is the study of home, which is to say the study of belonging. Though they have never seen a sperm whale, a blue whale, or a narwhal, something in their art helps my children connect to the world and their places in the universe, to the story that was and is and has always been. This connection, of course, can only ever happen on a creaturely level. There is no void, and thus no room for abstraction.

I have tried to approach this work in a similar manner, as a little child drawing whales, which is to say as an amateur. My work has benefitted from the work of ecologists, certainly, though I am not an ecologist in any professional sense. But I am, like everyone, woven into an ecology, a study of home, of belonging, a story about abiding here.

Fatherhood and faith are not the only means by which I have accessed this story and tried to understand my place in it, but it is difficult to name any others as personally significant. Simply put, becoming a father woke me to parts of the story that had for so long been obscured by shallow interpretations of faith—a word I use here broadly, as a stand-in for spiritual and religious consciousness, not necessarily in relation to any particular faith system.

I do, however, hesitantly identify as a Christian—perhaps as a mystic Christian, in the sense of being a seeker—or an earthly Christian, a human Christian, a Christian of the humus, of the loam, of the compost, a Christian of story, of art, of connection. What I mean by all this will hopefully be made clear, or at least clearer, in the pages that follow. But suffice it to say for now that I am of a time, a place, and a culture in which faith is a defining force, in some cases *the* defining force; it is something that has shaped me from infancy on. For the longest time, I took so much of it for granted.

After finding Thoreau, I began wrestling with it. Faith became my angel at Penuel—something I respected for what it was, something for which I'd sleep on a rock until it visited me, but something I could not let degrade my sense of empathy, creativity, or collective humanity. I was twenty-two, somewhere in Virginia on the Appalachian Trail, when I more or less realized this, though that is a story for another time.

When my children came along, I saw God. This was not the cartoon God I understood when I was a child as a bearded deity enthroned in heaven, or the fundamentalist's God who I'd been told had destroyed the world and would do it again, or the abstract God I wrestled on a rock on the Appalachian Trail five years before my first child was born. Rather, the God I met in my children was shaking, blue, covered in blood and fluid, and looked like their mother and me—a God who could be human. This is the same God who now sits drawing whales. This is the God who "plays in ten thousand places, lovely in limbs, and lovely in eyes not his," as Gerard Manley Hopkins put it. This is the God I seek with all that I am.

ꙮ

I wrote most of the words that have become this book between 2009 and 2014. The two notable exceptions are the essays "Reckoning These Ruins" and "Of War and the Red-Tailed Hawk," which I began drafting in the early summer of 2015. This book, then, is a rumination on my life and thought roughly from the time I learned I was going to be a father up until my son was five and my daughter three.

I suppose the best way to define this work is to say it is part essay collection, part memoir, part notebook. It might be less helpful but more meaningful to say it is a collection of chronicles, psalms, jeremiads, and visions. Whatever the case, the essays in the first and second sections, from "Phos Hilaron" to "Of War and the Red-Tailed Hawk," are more or less chronological. The poems dispersed throughout the book, of course, are not, at least not in relation to the essays. And the third section is something else entirely.

The third section of this book, which gives it the "part notebook" distinction and causes me to stumble and murmur when asked what the book is about, is not really chronological at all, whether in relation to itself or the two preceding sections. This final section does represent a story of sorts, and it is set against a timeline, but it is more associative than narrative, more patchwork than linear, more roughly seamed than fused, something like a quilt.

This third section, this quilt, was more or less finished in 2012. It predates the second section of the book and even some of the first. I've spot-cleaned it a couple times and gone back and fixed a fray or two, but I haven't added any entirely new patches or woven any new threads. The reason for this, I hope, will be clear enough by the end.

Even so, I should say that the quilt would be much larger if I were to try and make it today, but I suppose that is the nature of any published art, whether blanket or book. It would certainly include more scenes with my daughter, who was on her way but not yet born when I finished this section a little over four years ago. And I acknowledge that in the third section of this book there are events I have omitted in certain discussions on violence and injustice that would be present had I written the section four months ago rather than four years ago.

Over the past few years, since finishing what is the third section of this book, I have continued to learn and listen, and in so doing have become much more aware—though still not aware enough—of the pervasive violence and injustice at the core of a white, patriarchal structure that too often passes as Christian but is in reality far from it. This is the structure behind the disregard for the lives of people of color. It is the structure behind misogyny. It is the structure behind the continued discrimination against and contempt for LGBTQ people. It is the structure dependent on the othering of people of other faiths and those who identify by no faith at all. It is the structure that only cares for those who uphold it.

I wish this book to be, inasmuch as possible, a testament against that structure, part of the "single garment of destiny" and "inescapable network of mutuality" that Dr. King talked about. This, of course, is a life's work, and I am grateful for those whose work has enriched and continues to enrich my own, and to my wife and children who have woken me to a deeper sense of empathy in pursuing this work.

When my children were drawing whales at their art table this morning, my daughter had her blanket with her. This blanket—a small afghan quilt made by my wife's cousin—is practically an extension of my daughter's body. Her elbow rested against it as she drew her sperm whale and the rainbows through which Leviathan danced. This book is perhaps a blanket like that—something to rest an elbow upon while continuing in the real work, a start of what this work might become.

We know very little about sperm whales, and often speak of their abode as an abyss, a void. Yet surely, as in my daughter's picture, hidden well away from us, they swim in filtered light, shimmering, however far beneath the surface.

—Acworth, Georgia
April 2016

Prelude

Northbound on Old 41, I pass a church
I've passed for years—Blue Springs Primitive Baptist,
resting between the highway and high school parking lot.

A board hangs out front, says *Singing tonight*.
I think how I'd like to join them, if I could, how I'd like
to take my son with me, now drifting to sleep
in his car seat behind me, how we'd both love
to sing if matters of belief were of no consequence.

It would come down to this, I know:
I do not believe in the resurrection of Christ,
in the sense that he just up and walked from the grave
only to ascend and wait to return for the world's last war.
I do not believe in the flame that, some say, awaits sinners,
unbelievers, doubters and seekers, followers of other faiths.
I do not believe in sin or salvation, in the righteousness of the
          chosen,
the fallenness of creation, the inherent corruption of the
          world.

I believe that God is going to sleep
in the seat behind me, and that is all.
They might tell me I am wrong once they found out.
Even so, I imagine turning my car, waiting for the evening
song, for a thousand tongues to sing in communion
with this small congregation, a remnant people
in a remnant place, losing ground.

Part I: This Gladdening Light

The man old in days will not hesitate to ask a small child
seven days old about the place of life, and he will live.

—Gospel of Thomas

Phos Hilaron

I guess you could say I'm scared. Not so much because it's nightfall and I'm lost in the Smoky Mountains backcountry in a downpour, but because come December—just six months away—I'm going to be a father.

I've got five miles or so already behind me, no telling how many to go, no map, wondering whether the ranger I spoke to gave me bad directions to the campsite or if I just misunderstood her. *Didn't I pass that rock already? And how do I plan on raising a child if I can't even follow simple directions in the most frequently visited national park in the country?* A strap on my pack breaks, and the sudden shift in weight sends me stumbling through a rising, root-woven rill. The rain picks up with the rumbling of a charcoal sky. *I'm going to be a father.*

I let those words soak in with the rainwater soaking my shirt and socks and pack and everything else. I stop to fix the strap, cussing, fumbling around in the mud and darkness. *I'm going to be a father.*

ॐ

Tradition tells that the ancient Christians of Jerusalem kept a lamp burning in Christ's empty tomb, and at times of worship and celebration, they would venture out to the tomb, light a candle by the perpetual flame, and use it to illuminate their gathering place. They called this flame *phos hilaron.* Gladdening light. Hilarious light. But there's no such light here on this night in the Smokies—just an unseasonably cold rain, a worry in my heart, and a dense darkness settling among the hemlocks.

It strikes me that I should've thought this through a little better. There were ambulances at the trailhead, for Christ's sake. When I pulled up earlier, just before the rain set in, rangers were stationed in the parking area orchestrating an emergency rescue for a park visitor who'd injured herself tubing down the creek.

About a quarter-mile in I passed the convoy of trucks that had gone back far as the trail would allow to rescue the tuber. She was in a stretcher in a truck bed, accompanied by a number of paramedics perched on the wheel wells, heads ducked to avoid outstretched rhododendron branches. Several rangers were leading the way back to the graveled parking lot where half the Bryson City fire department was waiting. I didn't get a clear look at the tuber or hear exactly what happened, but I saw the swollen, rocky, deadfall-snagged creek, and could imagine.

Lowering my gaze in an awkward expression of deference for the injured party, I stepped off the trail so the cavalcade could pass, just as the rain began splattering through the forest canopy. That's when a rosy-cheeked, baldheaded ranger caught sight of me.

"Where you headed?" he grunted from his window, stopping his truck and halting the procession.

"Campsite 60," I said. "Ranger back there told me it's about three miles up the way, right at the fork."

"You by yourself?"

"Yessir."

"Got a permit?"

"Yessir," I said, fumbling through my pockets for my receipt. "I dropped it in the box back past the trailhead."

"So you're all by your lonesome?"

"Yessir," I said again, still digging in my pockets.

"So you're camping out all by yourself—on a night like this?"

"Yessir, I am. Everything okay?"

"Okay, I guess."

He glanced at the driver of the truck behind him and gave a little nod, as though signaling he'd approved my clearance. Then he nodded at me in the same manner, easing off the brakes, preparing to lead the injured lady back to civilization.

૭

A few miles, mud puddles, and mountains later, I come upon a familiar rock, veiled with the same mosses and ferns I admired the first time I passed, and soon realize I don't know where the hell I'm going. But just as I'm about ready to pitch my tent in the middle of the trail and risk a citation should any ranger pass by, I notice a signpost through the mist.

Deep Creek Trail, reads the sign, with an arrow pointed to the right. A couple hours ago I bore right onto Indian Creek Trail, which I now understand was not the fork I was supposed to take.

I head up the mountain alongside Deep Creek, sloshing all through the muck, surveying the dusk around me for a place to camp. Before too long I spot a clearing in the middle of a rhododendron thicket adjoining the creek. Stepping off the trail to get a closer look, I see a fire ring and a nice level spot for a tent blanketed with pine needles. The only thing missing is any indication that this is

Campsite 60, but at this point I don't care. I pitch my tent in the rain and sit down on a log, hoping to gather my thoughts before settling in for the night.

The chill and the weather and the unfamiliarity of this place lead to a somber mood, which leads to worry. I begin to think about my wife, who is back at home just north of Atlanta, two hundred or so miles from this rainy Appalachian hollow in western North Carolina. I am on my way to Vermont, stopping to camp this first night to save some money and enjoy a walk before a couple long days on the road, the first of many nights that I'll be away from her and our unborn child.

This realization brings misgivings about my trip north, and I begin to feel sorry that I ever left home in the first place. This sort of self-doubt and its attendant fear are quite familiar to me, and now that I've set camp and no longer have to worry about hiking around in the sodden darkness, I have time to mull them over. In doing so, I realize with a child on the way—no, with a child *here*, just hidden and protected within water, behind layers of muscle and bone and skin—that these wisps of doubt and fear are much more acute. How am I, who still so often feels like an insecure, scared child, going to raise a child to be secure and unafraid?

I find the moment overwhelming.

Soon my child will come into a world that, so I've been told, is fallen. That the world is fallen is a belief I am shedding, but to do so in light of daily exposures to violence—whether firsthand or through the various media outlets—is a difficult thing indeed. Because I worry so deeply about the world—a world I love and find essentially good, though it is being overrun by people bent on poisoning and destroying it—I worry all the more about my child who will soon enter it.

I've read that about two in a hundred babies born each year in America could have been exposed to enough mercury in utero to cause lifelong brain damage, and that, in my child's umbilical cord right now, there are likely to be traces of hundreds of industrial chemicals that have invaded the sanctuary of the womb, some of which may have disabling or life-ending potency. I do not understand how some cannot find it within themselves to care about even this, let alone the mountains just northwest of here, razed for coal to fuel power plants from which mercury seeps like blood, and into the blood of fish, the blood of human beings, the blood of mothers, the blood of unborn children.

If this will all be redeemed by Christ's blood, I don't know. I've already been told that I should accept what I once so readily did—heaven and hell, lost and saved, and all the other old dualities—to prepare myself for fatherhood. They wonder how I'll be able to raise a child of sound spirit when I am so unsure of my own spirituality. They ask what I plan to teach my child. Yet these woods speak, too, and in hushed tones still the waters speak.

ᴄ

On my mossy seat, with Deep Creek murmuring by, I settle into the rain, chewing on these thoughts and a granola bar, having given up altogether my attachment to a good night's sleep. I figure I ought to hang up my food so bears won't raid my camp later, but I have no rope in my pack, and, as this is probably not Campsite 60, there are no lines or posts for hanging food. So I take the bungee cord from around my sleeping pad, find two white pines about five feet from one another, and rig my food sack between them in such a way that's probably good for nothing but to give the bears a better view of it. The sky opens up again, and what was a steady rain becomes a deluge.

"The rain I am in," wrote the Trappist monk Thomas Merton from the porch of his hermitage in the Kentucky hills, "is not like the rain of cities. It fills the woods with an immense and confused sound...And I listen, because it reminds me again and again that the whole world runs by rhythms I have not yet learned to recognize, rhythms that are not those of the engineer."

I remember hearing my baby's heartbeat for the first time, the day we went in for my wife's first sonogram. An unexpected feeling came over me when I heard it, a feeling of needing to cry but not being able. Whether I was unable to cry because the sound came amplified through an engineered machine, or because a nurse who I did not know was in the room with us, or some other reason, I cannot say. But I do know that I heard my baby's heartbeat, which, like this rain, is a rhythm I have not yet learned to recognize. Like this rain, it tells me to be still and know. I will spend the rest of my life learning to hear it for what it is.

Presently the rain eases and I return to my log seat to finish off a peanut butter sandwich before calling it a night. From the woods beyond the trail, I think I see the flash of an approaching headlamp, and immediately recall my encounter with Ranger Fife back near the trailhead. I rattle off all my sins in my mind—*setting camp in an unauthorized spot, improperly storing my food sack, camping out all by my lonesome on a night like this*—trying to summon a defense for each. But then I see another flash, and another, and soon the misty forest is filled with the pale green light of blinking fireflies, like holy ghosts emerging from the hollows.

I notice another light, this one emanating from beneath a cluster of ferns across my camp. I stuff the last bite of sandwich in my mouth, leave the log for a closer look, move the ferns to the side, and there, atop the rotting forest floor, illuminating a fern canopy with an emerald radiance, I see one of the strangest and most beautiful creatures I've ever seen. It is a larviform adult female of the family *Phengodidae*—a glowworm beetle—curled around tiny eggs, protecting them from nocturnal predators, its light unwavering. To this creature, taking its light from beneath a bushel does not amount to an exercise in preaching or a means of saving souls, but is a measure to stay alive, and to keep its young alive. It is an instinctive act of belonging to the world. Had I a small enough book, I could read by such a light.

᷎

Minutes pass before I realize that I'm on my hands and knees on the damp earth watching this glowworm. Of course I know it's just an insect, however radiant it may be. I have seen plenty of insects in my life that I did not pause to consider. And of course this particular insect—though I'm sure it's aware of my presence—knows nothing of the wonder it has stirred in me, much less of how it's got me thinking of parenthood and religion, of how I find its literal light far more heartening and practical than much of the artificial light spread by industrial Christianity. Whether I'm a ridiculous man lying on the ground or a hungry skunk snuffing through the underbrush probably doesn't matter much to this beetle—I'm a potential threat and I'm sure it wants me gone.

But still something vital is happening here. No longer am I the troubled man on the log dreading a long, cold night away from my pregnant wife; rather, I'm acting somewhat like a child, huddled among dripping ferns looking at a creature I'd only read about before, not so much oblivious to the chilly mist and the forest floor as part of them.

After a while I retire to my tent for a little reading. A couple chapters in, I set the book aside and turn off my headlamp, settling into my sleeping bag and the cadence of chattering insects, the psalm of the gurgling creek. It is cool and damp but soon the tent warms and the possibility of sleep seems less remote. I wonder what Christ meant when he said that to enter the kingdom of heaven we must become as little children—an idea brimming with new meaning for me as a soon-to-be father. If we take heaven to be a supernatural realm dotted with mansions and crisscrossed by golden roads that we'll get to in the next life (so long as we say some version of a "sinner's prayer" in this one), I don't suppose crawling like a fool among a ferny creek bank is going to get anybody any closer to it. But if the kingdom of heaven is within us and in our midst, a thing to abide in here and now, I imagine becoming like children in a very pragmatic sense is the only way to fully enter it. There is heaven here beneath the hemlocks.

Every so often I look out the tent flap to see if the beetle is still aglow there beneath the ferns; I will be in dreams by the time this gladdening light fades. Droplets from the needles and leaves of the treetops above gather and descend in intermittent patters upon my tent. I rest unhindered at the doorstep of a sanctuary, as does my child in the timbre of his mother's heartbeat, miles and miles from these mountains. The clouds diffuse into milky wisps, like estuaries for the foundling stars, and I sleep. Truly there are lights in this world the darkness has not understood.

Formed by Water

...in a book I read and cherish,
Going to Walden is not so easy a thing
As a green visit. It is the slow and difficult
Trick of living, and finding it where you are.
                    —Mary Oliver, "Going to Walden"

The finest workers in stone are not copper or steel tools, but the
gentle touches of air and water working at their leisure with a
liberal allowance of time.
                    —Henry David Thoreau,
          A Week on the Concord and Merrimack Rivers

From its headwater spring on the wooded slopes of Rocky
Mountain in north Georgia, the Hiawassee River wanders
to a valley watched by the Appalachians. The mountains
brood over the river like herons and are as blue. Silver light
flickers in the mist; the mist dances through the air, drifting like shed feathers of these ancient water birds. The slate
wings of the mountains cast shadows on the river. Deana
and I stand ankle-deep in the water, seeking rocks.

We are here looking for a place to have our wedding
and have found a diversion in the cold river. We're after
rocks that resemble animals, though we will pick up any
rock that whispers to us, any rock whose smallest grain of
peculiar beauty catches our eyes.

We call this "rocking"—an idea borrowed from my
grandfather. We'd gone down to visit him and, as is customary in pleasant weather, the three of us sat in rusty lawn
chairs under his carport talking about matters broad as religion and politics, particular as horseshoes and the birds at

his feeder. During a lull in the conversation, Papa pointed to a rock resting by the driveway. "Look at that rock out yonder," he said, "and tell me what you think it looks like."

So we looked and pondered and finally Deana said: "Looks like a turtle to me."

The old man shifted in his chair, his lanky body folding into it just so. He grinned a half-grin. "Yep," he said, "it's a turtle."

He was proud—proud that he had a rock that looked like a turtle, and proud that Deana had answered correctly. He loved that rock and he loved Deana; he always called her his "country girl." When Deana went inside to get some water, Papa told me that if I didn't ask her to marry me soon, he'd ask her for me.

Deana rejoined us and we all talked more about that rock, the rock with the cathedral-dome shell, the curious eyes and slanted mouth, the clawed foot that perchance would become flesh in the cover of night and drag the stony creature to water. We asked Papa where he found it and he told us he'd hauled it from the creek down the road.

So now Deana and I seek rocks wherever a creek or river runs to shape the stones. Some rocks we just admire and set back in the water; some we keep for ourselves. We give Papa the ones that resemble animals to see if he can figure out what they are.

Rocking is a sacred thing to Deana and me, an enactment of the great pageant of creation in which nothing is happenstance. When Christ tells the Pharisees that even the rocks will cry out in praise if men fall silent, we believe it—we have *heard* it.

And so here we stand, the cold water of the Hiawassee flowing over our feet and ancient rocks. The rocks flow into the faces of animals. The faces of animals flow into our hands. Our hands overturn rocks beneath the water and will flow into union. Our union will flow into a child. Our child will flow into water, water into rocks, rocks back to faces. Her face is soft, nearly heart-shaped and framed by her dark hair.

In the cold water of the Hiawassee, a small rock rests among the others. I pick it up with the aim to skip it to the opposite bank to prove to Deana that I can, but end up holding on. It is a pretty rock, a blunt triangular shape, pale orange as an autumn oak leaf, streaked in ivory and silver. I put it in my pocket, and from my pocket place it in the car, there to forget it for a while.

᧖

It is the early summer of 2009, a little more than a year since Deana and I were married, not quite two years since we last stood in the Hiawassee River.

We've spent the last couple days exploring the Maine coast and now are on the road to Concord, Massachusetts—to Thoreau country. Ever since reading *Walden* years ago, I've wanted to come here, and this New England road trip with Deana, a "babymoon" of sorts, affords the perfect opportunity to visit.

In 1872—ten years after Thoreau died, his ten-by-fifteen cabin long since vanished—Bronson Alcott visited Walden and left a rock near the cabin site, thus starting a cairn in Thoreau's honor. That cairn is now a place of pilgrimage, and it is customary, I've heard, for those who cherish *Walden* to leave a rock of their own while at the pond. Walt Whitman and E.B. White left rocks on the pile, as have untold others moved by Thoreau's words. Ever since hearing of this tradition, I've wanted to do the same, and have brought a rock for that purpose: a blunt, triangular one, pale orange as an autumn oak leaf, streaked in ivory and silver.

ɕ

By the time we reach the outskirts of Concord, we're tired. Deana is particularly tired. And hungry. She is three months pregnant, after all.

I am new at this and have yet to learn that after ten hours on the road with a pregnant woman, one's chief obligations include finding a restroom, a place to eat, and a place to stay for the night—not turning onto the dark, woodsy road that leads out of town toward Walden Pond.

"Can't we just go get something to eat?" Deana says as I head toward the pond.

"Yeah, sure," I say. "Just a minute."

"Well, it's late," she says, "and you don't even know where you're going."

"Yeah, I do."

"No, you don't. That map we got at the rest stop isn't going to tell you where that rock pile is or whatever it is you're looking for."

"I just want to see the pond for a second."

"I'd rather just turn around. You don't know where you're going and we don't know where we're staying tonight. We need to find a hotel and eat. We can go sightseeing tomorrow."

"*Sightseeing?*" I say. "You think I want to go *sightseeing?*"

"Yes," she says. "What am I supposed to call it? We'll go sightseeing all day tomorrow. Will you please turn around?"

"You know I've been dreaming of coming up here for years," I tell her, "and you're ruining it."

She crosses her arms and looks out the window.

"Look," I say, "if we were visiting the Holy Land and went to see Jesus' empty tomb, would you call that 'sightseeing'? Wouldn't you want to go before you did anything else? That's the only way I know to explain it to you." I turn the car around, acting like I'm the one that's been put upon.

"A little band of dedicated Thoreauvians," writes E.B. White in an essay on his admiration for Thoreau, "would be a sorry sight indeed." White goes on to describe this Thoreauvian band as one made up of "fellows who hate compromise and have compromised," of "fellows who love wildness and have lived tamely." Add me to that sorry band, under the heading of "fellows who have compared Thoreau to Christ to make their pregnant wives feel badly for caring more about eating and sleeping than carelessly driving out toward Walden Pond at nightfall." But I will not admit it now.

A Best Western looms over the highway, so I pull in. I'm still putting on airs and Deana's still mad and I imagine we are a sight indeed walking into the lobby. Deana asks the receptionist for a room with two double beds. She takes the keys and heads to the room while I go move the car and haul up our luggage. Thus ensconced, and still in silence, we wander out to find a bite to eat.

Ichabod's Tavern is the only place open, so we park and head in. Despite its superficial nods to the '76er American spirit, the bar is a little tacky and upscale. Thoreau wouldn't have approved—but I don't tell Deana. They have food and that's all she cares about, and if it will put her in a better mood, then that's all I care about, too. And if it will not put her in a better mood, at least they have Sam Adams on tap.

I order a pint and make some reference to Dave Chappelle's Sam Jackson beer spoof to lighten the mood. Deana doesn't care much for the joke, so we just brood over our bad, expensive bar food in silence, feigning interest in the Red Sox game on the three televisions. Seeing John Smoltz in a Boston uniform instead of an Atlanta one doesn't help things.

Then we hear a familiar sound straight from Georgia: a jangled Peter Buck guitar riff followed by the crowing of Michael Stipe as R.E.M.'s "Pop Song 89" plays out over the speakers. That is our song—it has been ever since I put the *Green* album in the car stereo on one of our first dates and Deana made fun of the lyrics, *"Should we talk about the weather? Should we talk about the government?"* It's not my favorite R.E.M. song by any means but I couldn't have asked for a better one at the moment. I look across the table at Deana and she looks at me and breaks a hesitant smile, which starts in her brown eyes and slowly moves across her face.

We sit and discuss neither the weather nor the government, but make our plans for the morning, and talk, as we always do, about what we will name our baby.

‿

Morning breaks pleasantly through the window of our room at the Concord Best Western. I walk out to the car to get Deana's shower stuff and other bags I forgot to bring in, happy that we've waited to visit Walden today instead of trying to rush in last night. A cool breeze streams through the hotel parking lot beneath a cloudless sky. I have to admit: It is a perfect day for sightseeing.

After a short drive out Route 126, we arrive at a fee station, about the size of the replica of Thoreau's hut across the street. I give my $5 parking fee to the young man working the station and ask him how he's doing. He nods.

For some reason I am very aware of my Southern accent. I try my best to be proper, for this kid—though he doesn't know it and probably even hates his job—is about as close to St. Peter as I ever hope to see, here guarding the gates of Walden. He gives me a blue day-use pass that I am to display in my windshield.

"Whereabouts is the rock pile?" I ask.

"Rock pile? I'm not sure exactly what you mean," the kid says with a confused look.

I start to stammer and fidget in my seat. Deana rolls her eyes from the passenger side. "Chris, let's go," she says. "I've got to find a bathroom."

I reason that surely an employee of Walden Pond State Reservation would know about the rock pile. I wonder if I've given away some precious secret known only to Walden pilgrims; I worry that rock-leaving could be against the rules.

"Oh, sorry," I say to the young man. "Could you please point me in the direction of the original cabin site— Thoreau's, I mean? And where is the bathroom?"

"Who else could you have meant, Chris?" Deana says. "Just get a map and let's go. I'm about to pee my pants."

The kid hands me a map—basically a thick line going around what appears to be the pond. He points to the thick line.

"Just follow this trail," he says, "and turn right into the woods away from the beach to get to the cabin site. Restrooms are in the bathhouse by the beach."

I nod and thank him and hand the map to Deana.

"You're something else," she says.

The pond comes into view through a stand of pines, and then we see the bathhouse rising above a crowded beach.

"There it is," Deana says. "Hurry up!"

I turn on the road toward the bathhouse and park as close as I can.

༄

Noting the many ironies at Walden Pond today is, I imagine, an established cliché among readers of Thoreau. There is, for instance, the shop selling t-shirts for $20 each that, quoting *Walden*, say, "Simplify, simplify." There is a hot dog stand and an ice cream truck on the shores of a pond made famous by a man who ate mostly cornmeal and rice while living there (though taking that to an extreme has added to his myth, of course—he might've enjoyed a hot dog, for all I know). There is the busy beach with the lifeguard and all the noise and litter. And there are the signs that say, "Stay on the trail." ("Every path but your own," wrote Thoreau, "is the path of fate. Keep on your own track, then.")

Walden Pond is full of swimmers today. I hear them before I see them, and when I see the first one, I think I've seen some sort of wildlife—an otter, perhaps, or an enormous muskrat. But, on a closer look, the skullcap and goggles betray this bather as part of my tribe.

A travel brochure that Deana and I picked up at the Massachusetts Welcome Center says that "Walden Pond, which so inspired Henry David Thoreau, is as idyllic today as it was 150 years ago." That's a tad hyperbolic, I'm afraid. When I first read Thoreau's words in *Walden* that "You only need sit still long enough in some attractive spot in the woods that all its inhabitants may exhibit themselves to you by turns," I hardly envisioned a hairy old man in a Speedo emerging from the pond to sun himself on a rock.

Even in Thoreau's time, this pond was hardly "idyllic." Thoreau complained often of the noise of the train on the pond's far shore, of the clamor of carts and buggies on their way to Concord, of the businessmen who gathered Walden's winter ice to ship to Southern markets. As the poet Mary Oliver writes, going to Walden—whether you're Thoreau or anybody else—is no simple thing.

After the bathroom break, we roam into the woods, following the line on our map. I am walking ahead; Deana yells for me to wait and so I do. Turning around the next bend, we see a blue jay chick, soft and blue-white, hopping through pine needles, hollering for its mother. A chipmunk rushes from beneath a mossy log and pummels the chick—and pummels it again, and again. The chick rolls with each tackle, accumulating mud and pine needles like a dirty snowball, and continues its screeching.

In his journal for June 25, 1858, after watching a group of young chipmunks at play, Thoreau asked, "Who striped the squirrel's side?" I'd always thought it a rhetorical question; but now Deana and I watch the mother blue jay swoop down from on high and thrash the chipmunk, which gives an answer to Thoreau's riddle: the blue jay, in this case, striped the squirrel's side. The chipmunk starts for the chick once more, but the mother's aerial assault proves too much, and the chipmunk retreats to its log.

Witnessing the battle of the chipmunk and the blue jay places me in the story of this forested shore. I recall a passage from *Walden* in which Thoreau describes a battle between two tribes of ants—one red, the other black— comparing the ants' struggle to the Trojan War: "The legions of these Myrmidons," he writes, "covered all the hills and vales of my wood yard, and the ground was already strewn with the dead and dying, both red and black." Such a thing happened in these very woods. And in these very woods, such things happen still—the blue-jacketed jay and the dusty gray ground squirrel still waging their unfinished campaign here among these shadowy trees, perhaps farther north than one would think, where the world will never see it.

The map says we're getting closer: It appears the hut site is just on the other side of this cove that extends a good ways into the woods. The trail winds through a thicket beside a swampy section of the pond and we squish our way along. I step upon a raised plank stretching across an expanse of mud, where water trickles from the pond into this isolated cove to the right—Thoreau's cove. I wait for Deana and take her hand as we cross the narrow board to the other side.

"How many a man," wrote Thoreau, "has dated a new era in his life from the reading of a book!" Reading *Walden*

five years ago—just about the time that I met Deana—
began my new era.

I could be a purist about it and say that *Walden* was
and is like my Bible, that five years ago it became the primary text of my spirituality. But I know where that leads—
to overzealous talk about Thoreau and Jesus, to tears and a
spoiled supper. Purism tends to preclude the needs of others, as it did when I lost my head for a minute and went
driving this way last night, without a care in the world for
my pregnant wife, as though this pond were a magnetic
shrine. In *Walden*, Thoreau wondered how people "can live
this slimy, beastly life, eating and drinking." Run that one
by Deana, Henry, and let me know how it works out.

But the biblical comparison is fair within limits. Thoreau wrote that "the morning wind forever blows, the poem
of creation is uninterrupted; but few are the ears that hear
it." It is that understanding of creation as poetry—an understanding that absolutely permeates *Walden*—that spoke
to me so when I first read the book. This created world,
this very ground I tread, is a poem, and one in which I get
to partake. I think E.B. White gave the best one-line description of *Walden* when he said it is "like an invitation to
life's dance."

I was troubled back when I first cracked the book's
pages—worried over my family and my place in the world,
and these worries informed my early relationship with
Deana. Thoreau's words, of course, did not magically cure
my troubles, but they did, and still do, inform me of the
true substance of these things. "Shams and delusions are
esteemed for soundest truths," writes Thoreau, "while reality is fabulous." That passage spoke to me when I was twenty-two, and it speaks to me still at twenty-six, here on this

board straddling Walden Pond's edge, my wife a step behind me, her hand in mine, the cold sapphire water of a New England glacial pool to our left, boggy cove water to our right, the restful water within her, our child's hands within that water, our hands seeking rocks beneath it all. We three together wander amid this fabled reality.

∾

The author of Genesis tells a story of Jacob fleeing his brother, Esau, who plotted to kill him, for Jacob had tricked Esau out of their father's inheritance. On his journey through the desert to the Euphrates River, Jacob stops for the night, lays his head on a stone, and falls asleep. He dreams he sees a ladder "set up on the earth, and the top of it reached to heaven: and behold the angels of God ascending and descending on it." From atop the ladder, the God of Abraham and Isaac calls down and blesses Jacob.

Jacob wakes, whispering, "Surely the Lord is in this place; and I knew it not"; he proclaims that the patch of dirt upon which he had slept is "none other but the house of God, and this is the gate of heaven." At first light, Jacob takes the stone he had used for a pillow and pours oil on it, and names the place Bethel—"house of God."

There is nothing striking about the wooded cove when Deana and I reach the other side of the footbridge—just a stand of white pines and young maples and oaks with some rhododendron and other leafy undergrowth. Deana notices the rock pile first and shows it to me. Beside the rock pile is a small rectangular cluster of granite pillars linked by a chain—Thoreau's hut site. There is nothing within the chain's border, hardly any evidence that a foundation was ever there. From the site, a wide, dusty, well-worn path meanders down to the pond's edge.

I take the river rock from my pocket and set it with the others. I arise and whisper my thanks in a breeze that floats off the water and rustles the leaves. Deana notices my eyes, which I'd tried to wipe with my sleeve, and puts her arm around me. We stand there at the edge of the rock pile and look out to the pond. To imagine angels ascending and descending on a ladder in our midst would not be a hard thing to do; but no imagination is needed. There in front of us are the ordinary white pines, rooted in the earth, their tops reaching to heaven, ascended and descended by woodpeckers and a red squirrel. I had always imagined being alone on my first trip to Walden, of sitting on the shore all day and reading Thoreau's words. But Deana's presence is my blessing, a confirmation that here is the gate of heaven through which we ever walk.

With a last look around, we turn and head back down the trail, talking of where we might get a bite to eat back in Concord. Before returning to the car, we walk across the street to the Walden Pond store—the one I'd scoffed at earlier—for a look around. Deana loves Christmas ornaments, and we collect them from special places we visit; and, sure enough, this shop has them. We buy a Walden ornament and a children's book for our baby about a mouse who lived with Thoreau.

Hundreds of miles south of here lie mountains blue as the wings of herons. Where the birds sleep in their misty rookeries, a river forms rocks to faces. As Thoreau writes, "I must now walk where I can see the most water, as to the most living part of nature. This is the blood of the earth, and we see its blue arteries pulsing with new life now." I hope this water will fashion our child's face after Deana's, for she is beautiful.

Original Sound

What is important in the child is his primal utterance, his response to *being*, his own free cries and signs, his admiration.
    —Thomas Merton, *Conjectures of a Guilty Bystander*

I hear the sound I love, the sound of the human voice...
    —Walt Whitman, "Song of Myself"

In the beginning was the electric noise of a sonogram, a hum fluttering in my ears, drowning out all else, not from decibel force, not from loudness, but from its soft yet demanding call to listen: the kind of call that attends the murmur of half-sleep, the momentary vibrations of moth wings on a windowpane, the embracing and pulsating silence beneath a still river pool surrounded by rapids and falls, echoing granite. The nurse told us that was our child's heartbeat.

⚮

Months later we hung ornaments from the doorframes, twelve little stained glass disks, each depicting one of the twelve days of Christmas. Deana was grumpy and uncomfortable but still she hung them carefully, ritually. The ornaments from her childhood dangled from multi-colored thumbtacks and spun in dim light.

Our families were on their way for Christmas Eve supper. I was putting together last-minute gifts as they arrived: reindeer made of logs from the backyard, branches for antlers, sweet gum balls nailed down for noses, using the washing machine and dryer as sawhorses. I'd seen someone selling these ornamental reindeer for $25 each at a roadside stand and figured I could make them myself. I cut into one of the logs and termites poured from their hollow abode onto the floor. I swept them from mudroom into the cold yard.

Soon our house was full—sisters, brother, parents, in-laws, dogs. Deana got hot and set the thermostat low and soon people complained of being cold. I put on long sleeves and those who were the coldest retrieved their jackets.

My brother-in-law took a phone call and held the top of the hallway doorframe as he spoke. "No, no, not labor yet, just little contractions," he said into the phone. He knocked down the ornament with a picture of a maid-a-milking and it shattered on the wood floor. Deana glared at him and turned the heat down one more notch. I poured myself a couple beers into a tall handmade stein that I bring out for special occasions. And this certainly was one: Christmas Eve, my son on the way. A New Year's birthday, maybe.

Deana glared at me, too. In retrospect, she had a strong feeling, or probably knew, that I'd be driving later, through the rain, to the hospital. But the way I saw it, the Braxton Hicks contractions had been going on for several days; what was to say they would not go on for several more? I swigged my beer, sat back in my chair, and thought what a pleasant Christmas Eve it was.

ॐ

Everyone left after supper, except for my in-laws who were staying with us through the holidays, and things got a little quieter. I was sitting in the dining room having one last beer with my brother-in-law when I heard the moaning down the hall. It was rather awkward sitting there with my brother-in-law at that moment, his sister's early labor moans reverberating through the house. He'd told me earlier in Deana's pregnancy that since Deana was pregnant, he knew we'd had sex, but he was okay with it. And so the beer helped.

Deana was sitting at the edge of our bed, still moaning, grimacing, holding her back with one hand and her belly with the other, rocking back and forth as I entered our room. This was no false labor contraction. I stood beside her, asked what I could do to help, and put my hand on her shoulder; she swatted it away. I waited. The contraction passed.

Our two dogs, both rescue mutts, followed at my heels. They whined and jumped on the bed beside Deana; Daisy sniffed her belly, Gracie licked her face, and both looked at me as though I knew what to do. On my way back to the kitchen to microwave a tube sock full of uncooked rice to put on Deana's back, I told my brother-in-law that it looked like our son would have at least one thing in common with Jesus. And I assumed he knew I was referring to a shared birthday and not to an immaculate conception.

✌

I started timing the contractions at about 10 P.M. and logged them all on the back inside cover of *What to Expect When You're Expecting* in scribbles that now seem hieroglyphic. Between contractions I rubbed Deana's back and held the hot rice sock to it; during the contractions I pressed her lower back to counteract some of her pressure and pain—pain that the King James Bible calls "sorrow"— offering my arms and hands for her to brace herself. She clenched my arms and leaned forward as the contractions came, our dogs keeping watch between us. On my next trip to the kitchen to warm up the rice sock, I realized that everyone in the house was awake, sitting, listening, waiting.

At 2 A.M., after a call to the hospital midwife, I threw some clothes in a bag and led Deana out into the cold rain and darkness of Christmas morning, her parents behind us, loading up their own car, my brother-in-law staying behind to watch the dogs. In the rearview mirror I watched as my father-in-law slipped on the soaked grass and slid down the hill to the street. After a few seconds he stood, his jeans and plaid shirt slicked in mud. I asked Deana if we should wait and she groaned and told me to go. And so I went.

Out on the interstate, the rain picked up and red lights flared and yellow lights shimmered and industrial wire Christmas trees shone blue and white from the tops of buildings. I called my parents and sisters and when I used the phrase "I'm fairly certain she's in labor," Deana yelled at me to hang up and drive. I hung up and drove, silence on the great highway but for tires treading wet asphalt, but for the cries of a lovely and hurting woman full of life, of life and sorrow, of sorrow and joy—of joy, somehow, unaccounted for.

ℐ

"In the massed crowd," writes Thomas Merton in a Christmas reflection called "The Time of the End Is the Time of No Room,"

> ...there are always new tidings of joy and disaster. Where each new announcement is the greatest of announcements, where every day's disaster is beyond compare, every day's danger demands the ultimate sacrifice, all news and all judgment is reduced to zero. News becomes merely a new noise in the mind, briefly replacing the noise that went before it and yielding to the noise that comes after it, so that eventually everything blends into the same monotonous and meaningless rumor. News? There is so much news that there is no room left for the true tidings, the 'Good News,' *The Great Joy*.
>
> Hence, The Great Joy is announced, after all, in silence, loneliness and darkness...

In silence we entered the hospital and signed the papers, and a kind nurse working such an awful shift that frigid Christmas morning checked us into a room and said the midwife on call was on her way. She told us that many of the mothers-to-be there had for some reason scheduled C-sections for Christmas morning, but that one poor woman had delivered her baby shortly after midnight in her car in the hospital parking lot.

෨

Sin, the dogma goes, is our inheritance from Adam. We are born into that inheritance, and so in that sense it is "original." We have only to enter the world, to float the channels of a natural process, and we are in sin, stained by it from infancy on.

We are not born into innocence, say the preachers; but Christ, being born of a virgin, *was* born into innocence. Thus they affirm the link between sin and sex, between sin and birth, between birth and the need for salvation.

ᔪ

I held a small trash can for Deana as she threw up, wiped the bile from her face and gown when she finished, and got her a bucket of ice chips. She wanted to have our son as naturally as is possible in a hospital, and so she pushed and labored for three hours after we arrived, the midwife holding one of her legs, me holding the other.

The midwife and the nurses whispered to each other, spoke in the hall. At about 5 A.M., they gave Deana an epidural. She shook, shivered, cried. A couple hours later, she started pushing again, threw up several times more as she was pushing, and the midwife told us the baby was not descending. Deana pushed until about 9 A.M., when the midwife said the baby still had not moved and that a C-section was needed to prevent an emergency, that our son's lungs were filling with amniotic fluid and meconium, that he was simply not going to come out on his own.

The nurses turned up Deana's epidural and pricked her with a needle until the anesthesiologist was convinced she was numb to the chest, and they gave me a set of blue scrubs.

ᔪ

"We are human," writes Thomas Merton, "and the only thing stopping us from living humanly is our own deeply ingrained habit of delusion, a habit which some of us stubbornly continue to associate with original sin."

୬

We are human. Deana was crying when I joined her in the operating room. I sat in a swivel chair by the table and held her hand and touched her face. Condensation and snot from my own tears clung to the inside of the surgical mask they'd given me.

The white antiseptic room, the silver steel machines, the failure to descend, pelvis too small, the curtain before the blood, lights above her wound, the time of the end, the time of no room. "Daddy, stand and see your boy."

I stood and looked over the curtain and saw them take him from her. They lifted him from the dark, from the sunrise and rain of the early morning, from burned and cut veins, cushion of organs. He was cold and trembling. She asked me what he looked like and I was trembling, too. I just said, "He's beautiful," but that did not account for it all.

Cannon was silent, not breathing, blue as a heron feather, though I did not tell Deana. I did not tell her that he looked to be gasping as I stood, holding her hand, watching the doctors laying him onto a table, placing a suction over his mouth. I went to him and took his hand and he held my thumb. The doctor turned on the machine. Some meconium rose but most did not and there was still no sound.

A few more times. A few more silences. And then he cried.

୬

"Shoulder your duds dear son, and I will mine," sings Whitman, "and let us hasten forth... Long enough have you dream'd contemptible dreams, / Now I wash the gum from your eyes, / You must habit yourself to the dazzle of the light and of every moment of your life." Hay and oxen, holy lights, cold and damp, visitations. I lost what little belief I still had in original sin that day.

I lost *belief*, too, lost it for *being*, for the reality and presence of the sorrow, the blood, the blue, the mother, the boy. He cried, she cried, and that was a voice calling. They cried and that was the first sound I really heard.

ço

Epilogue: Image

This waking to such an original sound was immediate, concrete. I did not have to wrestle any angels or wonder for a moment who I was. The room was a kind of vacuum where abstract thought and imposed structures had nothing at all upon which to cling or prey. It's not that I stopped believing in sin at that moment: Sin simply did not exist.

Reflecting on his ascent of Mt. Katahdin in *The Maine Woods*, Thoreau writes:

> ...here not even the surface had been scarred by man, but it was a specimen of what God saw fit to make this world. What is it to be admitted to a museum, to see a myriad of particular things, compared with being shown some star's surface, some hard matter in its home! I stand in awe of my body, this matter to which I am bound has become so strange to me. I fear not spir-

its, ghosts, of which I am one,— *that* my body might,—
but I fear bodies, I tremble to meet them. What is this
Titan that has possession of me? Talk of mysteries!—
Think of our life in nature,—daily to be shown matter,
to come in contact with it,—rocks, trees, wind on our
cheeks! The *solid* earth! the *actual* world! the *common*
sense! Contact! Contact! Who are we? *where* are we?

A wild mountain and a birth are not so different.
While a hospital operating room might seem the antithesis
of primordial wilderness, the contact there in that room
was fierce and immediate all the same—wilder in some
ways than a windswept Appalachian summit could be.

This birth, too, was a surface unscarred by man, "a
specimen of what God saw fit to make this world." And it
was a summit, an apex—feminine and fierce, violent and
fully innocent—that, unlike a mountain, I could never cross
over. It was not so much a moment for epiphany as a moment stripped to the core of things where the need for
epiphany, for revelation, for meaning, for interpretation
does not dwell. It was a moment of mother and child,
breath and sound, pain and release, uncorrupted and incorruptible being.

My clarity in that moment was not grounded in rock
and weather, but in the silence of a blue, trembling baby
and the pain of his mother, and the breaking of silence like
a storm when he cried. Once he cried, once he let his voice
be known and shattered this concept of sin like it were only
some joke passed along for thousands of years, the doctors
held him to Deana's face. She touched him a moment, he
held my finger a moment, and the doctors laid him in a
padded rolling cart to take him to the neonatal intensive

care unit and to prep Deana for her recovery. She told me to follow and stay with our son, so I did.

Those hours were a blur of oxygen masks, of windows, of following nurses through hallways, of reports about breathing and blood sugar, of changing diapers. I was there for him in the only way I knew to be.

But this is not a story about me. Soon after Deana was taken back to her room, the nurses gave her a picture of our son, an image in a Styrofoam frame decorated with Styrofoam candy canes, snowflakes, elves, and Christmas trees. She held this image close to her while I was away shadowing our son, and she was holding it to her chest when I returned to her room a couple hours later.

I would be able to hold him, still connected to his wires in the NICU, that evening; and she, after resting much more, would be able to visit the NICU with me in her wheelchair to hold him the next day.

When she held him, he looked into her face, and her face was a mirror, which had been from the beginning.

Walking the Whitetail

Water oak leaves crackle underfoot as I tread the faded green porch steps, child in my arms, into the light of late October.

A wren regards the boy and me from a scrap pile against the house, the thin woods about us distilling birdsong and the clamor of a howling train. I load up my son for a drive to Red Top Mountain State Park, just outside the town of Emerson among the rust-red foothills of northwest Georgia. It is a special day for us—the first of what I intend to be weekly outings for breakfast and hiking, just him and me.

Waffle House is already crowded by the time we get there, so we cross the interstate and head to the next one, less than a mile from the first and with no crowd at all. The folks sitting at the bar and the servers and cooks all smile and wave at my son and tell me what a precious thing he is; I thank them and try to get him to wave back, but he just grins and burrows his face against my shoulder.

I sit him in a highchair and order our breakfast. As we await our waffle, hash browns, and grits, an elderly woman stops to talk to my son, asking me his name. I tell her it is Cannon. She tells me what a handsome name it is, that it suits him, and wonders whether it is a family name. It's after his great-grandmother's maiden name, I reply, and she says just how pretty. She waves and says goodbye and baby-talks my son a little more on her way out. He watches her, eyes intent and dark, so soft a face breaking forth to smile for some inaudible hilarity, as though ghosts of those who've gone before him were whispering gladness in his ear.

Our breakfast arrives, and, as his buttery grits cool, I break bits of waffle for Cannon and drop the pieces before him as one would feed a sparrow. He takes the broken bread, smeared with syrup and butter, and tucks it bit by bit in his cheek, sucking his syrupy fingers all the while. This is new, feeding himself like this, the taste of syrup newer still. I feed him his grits in between waffle bites as I finish my own breakfast, and before too long we are full. The server who takes our check says she'd ask how everything was but for the grits and syrup on my son's face.

From the thick aroma of coffee and grease, the soft conversation and country music, my son and I head out into the cool air tinged with gasoline and exhaust, the engines rumbling from across the parking lot on Highway 92, and we join it all.

We approach Red Top from the east, winding through a series of abandoned strip malls and trailer parks, past small churches with names like Antioch Baptist Bible and Son-Shine Apostolic, past convenience stores marketing bait and tackle and cold beer, past car garages fenced in barbed wire, past campgrounds and boat ramps operated by the U.S. Army Corps of Engineers. Many of the roadside yards are filled with plastic gravestones for Halloween; all the roadside ditches are filled, for no holiday in particular, with plastic of one kind or another. To the west lie the mini-mansions, the yacht clubs, the gated communities on razed hillsides, some looming clear across the lake from gray patches in the autumn woods.

We cross the state park boundary not too long after passing the Dollar General and turn off the highway down a steep road toward the lake. Red Top Mountain State Park sits on nearly 2,000 acres of peninsula jutting into Lake Allatoona, a reservoir created by the damming of the Etowah River in the late 1940s. As part of the Flood Control Acts passed in the middle of the last century, the creation of Lake Allatoona—along with similar damming projects throughout the country—was managed from a distance by the War Department. Because the park's main draw is the lake and its shoreline, Red Top Mountain is perhaps as unnatural as state parks come.

Yet beauty endures. Despite the reservoir's violent beginnings, despite the troubled economic times that have visited this and all of Georgia's state parks, beauty endures, if in no other place than beneath a young tree in the middle of a landscaped island, in the parking lot where children are gathering leaves when Cannon and I pull up. I park, open the back door, and my son smiles a toothy smile, squinting as the sunlight dances across his face. I take out his off-road stroller and pack him up, placing a water bottle and a diaper in the basket under his seat, and I push my boy into the woods on the Whitetail Trail.

The Whitetail is short, traversing the length of a minor peninsula about a half-mile into the reservoir. We follow the trail as it dips into a cove along a dried-up rivulet full of weeds and saplings; the lake is low and has been for a while. The downhill portion of the trail slants crossways, approaching forty-five degrees at times. Cannon adjusts himself with each tip and turn and never makes a fuss.

The trail spills from the hilly forest to level ground at the lakeshore. We cross an old footbridge hugged by the roots of beeches and sweet gums; where these roots once rested in water, they now shine in caked mud like gasping catfish. All the water east of the bridge is gone. To the northwest, bare, brittle shores flicker in the sun until at last they melt into Allatoona.

We are folded into that which was and that which should not be—the ugly ground to the east where there is no water and was none before war men dammed the Etowah, the picture to the northwest where water remains where it never was. Tall white poles break from the lake to warn boaters of rocks and hills. We straddle the line between it all in the shadow of October trees, the tarnished copper leaves of the oaks, the ruby branches of dogwoods smoldering like once-flaming swords dropped and forgotten by some Edenic angel.

The trail ends on a pine bluff overlooking the choppy water. I park the stroller and pick up my son, who notices a lavender butterfly riding the breeze. He's only recently started noticing things so small. We sit for a minute on a rock and then I think it might be fun to take him down to the water's edge so he can crawl in the sand. Crawling is another recent discovery of his, and he has never really crawled outside, at least not on a sandy lakeshore—so that settles it.

I hold him as tightly as I can and together we scramble down boulders and rock pilings. His mother would have had a fit seeing us do it, but we make it safely to the sand without so much as a stumble. With the low water, the shoreline is wider than normal—if normal applies to a manmade lake—and has become a boneyard of pines. We find a soft spot amid the rocks and sit down as a speedboat sends ripples our way.

To Cannon, this place is new and I imagine his love encompasses it all—the noisy helicopter overhead no less than the water he watches in wonder. This is a holy place, scarred though it may be. We sit and breathe for a moment together, the breeze blowing his hair in a way that breaks my heart, his hands on my arm, we two looking out at the lake in the wind by which drift the smells of mussel beds and piney woods, of smoke and baby skin.

But he gets bored with the transcendental after a while—as he should—and crawls from my lap onto the red clay sand mixed with mica and shards of rock. He loves the sand, which he shows by flapping his arms and grunting. He props himself up against me and begins patting the ground.

Once he realizes the sand is pliable, he sticks his hands beneath it, sweeps it in his lap, squeezes it in his palms. On the tops of his hands are patterns that rise from beneath his skin, scarlet lines of pulsing blood that prove he is of my tribe though somewhat different, a little closer than me to the origin of things, far more innocent than men of my age.

If only I could think back so far, to my beginnings, to a time when my hands, too, were traced with so intricate a map penned by the maker of the world. I worry about this world, about my place in it, about what it will hold for my son. Perhaps I'm predisposed to pessimism, I don't know, but though I've shed my adolescent skin of Christian literalism, I can't help but think we've been banished from something altogether lovely and right and that we will just keep trying, with our wars and our industrial progress, to compensate for the fact that we don't know what this little boy putting dirty sand in his mouth knows.

My son swallows a little bit of that sand and I laugh. He finds it all funny, so he reaches down for another handful to put in his mouth, but I figure I'd better stop him this time. Eventually, he gives up the sand, flaps his arms like they are mallard wings, and starts to crawl. He hasn't crawled two feet before he finds a brown pine needle to play with; he reaches for it and holds it in the air, waving it this way and that.

After a while I pick my son up and we climb back to the bluff. A green anole rests on a pine clinging to a boulder beside the parked stroller. I hold my son out and he reaches for the lizard, grazing its tail as it retreats to a crevice.

My child is asleep well before we reach the footbridge, rocked in his stroller to the rhythms of roots. In the quiet of the woods, I think back to the shore, to my son swaying the pine needle, and I remember the Genesis story. It is a fine story, I suppose, for everywhere there is evidence of something awry, a kind of brokenness that is felt more than specified. We are never quite ourselves. Perhaps we are on the outside of an Eden, then, whether we have banished ourselves or been banished by God. I cannot say.

But the story of the Fall is one that has served its purpose, and walking the Whitetail as Cannon sleeps, I have a different vision. The entrance to paradise is not blocked by cherubim with a flaming sword; it is not blocked by anything. Rather, at the threshold of the garden there sits a little child, holding a pine needle, which he turns every way, bidding us enter.

Treasure This Ecstasy

[Winter Visitors]
(January 2011) Just outside my window, birds descend from the bare limbs of sweet gums and water oaks, visiting my feeder, gathering around the seeds I've strewn across the snow. I sit on the floor and watch them as Deana and Cannon sleep in the midmorning cold.

The dim light filters through clouds and reveals an array of wings and winter. The titmice and Carolina chickadees are constants most of the year but the weather this morning brings them in droves; they flit about the feeder hanging from the porch awning, sometimes clinging to icicles until a place at the feeder clears. The feathers of the titmice match the sky—wispy slate blue overcoming the gathering, rolling smoke-dark of the night's storm. The chickadees retain the shades of storm on their bodies, their midnight-black caps, their ice-gray wings and breasts.

Unlike the titmice and chickadees that will take their sunflower seeds and retreat to the trees to crack and eat them—alighting on the feeder but for a moment—house finches, gray-brown with traces of crimson, cover the feeder, eating their seeds on the spot, rarely moving until they've eaten seed after seed. They chatter in the gusts of wind and the advances of swifter birds.

Last night I set out extra blocks of suet—which I make myself with peanut butter, cornmeal, and leftover grease—knowing a snowstorm was stirring, a rarity here in the Georgia piedmont, and that the birds would need more energy to get through the coming days and nights. I put one of the suet cakes in a wire feeder and placed the extras on the porch rail. Chickadees and wrens visit the suet cage at times before proceeding to the seed feeder, and every so often I watch a downy woodpecker bob through the air, as though underwater, and latch onto the cage, which twists and sways with the bird's landing.

Deana stirs, opens our bedroom door, steps softly to the bathroom. Several bluebirds—as dull a blue as the season, approaching gray—descend on the porch rail to peck at the suet cakes with pine warblers and wrens, a procession of blue, pollen-yellow, and copper set against the snow and dingy white paint of the porch.

"After a still winter night I awoke with the impression that some question had been put to me, which I had been endeavoring in vain to answer in my sleep," wrote Thoreau in contemplation of Walden Pond in winter. As juncos, sparrows, and mourning doves gather on the ground to eat the seeds resting on top of the ice, and as a cardinal flickers in the deep green of a holly bush, I sense that same kind of somnolent question, which Deana wakes and puts to words: "Weren't you just talking about wanting Cannon to have a brother or sister?" she asks as she opens the creaking bathroom door, a pregnancy test in her hand.

[Caves]
The doctors told Deana and me that our daughter wouldn't turn on her own, that Deana wouldn't go into labor. This after other things: that our unborn daughter's kidneys had too much fluid in them, that there was too much space between her spine and her brain, that she was going to be very big—*macrosomic* was the word they used. It seemed that every appointment they would ask us about gestational dia-

betes, would ask Deana whether or not she had passed the test. She had. "Oh," they would say. "Just a big baby then."

The doctors told us not to worry about the macrosomic part. It would necessitate a C-section, they said, but otherwise there was no problem. For the extra fluid in our daughter's kidneys, and especially for the space between her spine and brain, the doctors ordered several sonograms and eventually, when those didn't provide clear enough images, an MRI.

I brought books with me to Deana's MRI appointment, as a nurse had suggested, given that it would take a good bit of time. We talked in the waiting room, Deana and I, both a little worried, both a little hopeful. When they called Deana's name, I decided I would not take the books in, so I went to put them and all our other things into the locker they gave us. As I was about to close the locker, a nurse asked me if I had anything to read. I pulled *The Brothers Karamazov* out of Deana's purse and took it into the machine-filled room, its great plastic cave in the middle.

Years before, not too long after we'd met, Deana took me caving at Raccoon Mountain, just outside Chattanooga. I only panicked once, trying to climb up through a tight crevice, unable to see where I was going, my slick boots slipping on a hill of pebbles and rock shards, no grip at all. But Deana was behind me, in the cave with me, there above a shallow pool, an abode of salamanders. I was not pregnant with a child or with fears for that child's health; I had the earth if nothing else, contact with the ground, the musty mud, and could lie down, gather myself, plunge upward once peace settled. ("Love to throw yourself on the earth and kiss it. Kiss the earth and love it with an unceasing, consuming love.") Deana's belly nearly touched the sides of the white tunnel as she entered. ("God took seeds from different worlds and sowed them on this earth, and His garden grew up and everything came up that could come up.") Soon noise drowned the room. I sat in my chair, wearing clunky earphones, cold, clutching my book like a rolled newspaper. ("But what grows lives and is alive only through the feeling of its contact with other mysterious worlds.") Deana panicked in the scanner, pressed the call button for the nurse, and came out crying. I put down my book, unopened and bent, and walked to Deana, kissed her forehead, gave her water. ("Water the earth with the tears of your joy and love those tears.") The nurse consoled her and, once Deana was calm, sent her back in the scanner. ("Treasure this ecstasy, however senseless it may seem to men.")

A few days later, we went back to the maternal fetal diagnostic center to talk about the MRI results. "You know how I told you I've only been wrong once in the past thirty years?" the doctor said. We nodded. "Well, I lied. I've been wrong many times. This is one of those times. Your baby's going to be fine. Big, but fine."

Deana got an automated call a day or so later telling us her C-section was scheduled for September 8, for us to be at the hospital by 5 A.M. with our paperwork.

§

"Is there any chance I'll go into labor on my own?" Deana asked her obstetrician at the next appointment, two weeks before the 8th.

"None. And in fact you don't want to. You'll still need a C-section no matter what, and if you do go into labor, go straight to the hospital. But you won't. She's not coming on her own."

Deana nodded, I nodded, and the doctor continued: "We're almost there, kiddo. You're almost there. I'll see you next week. How's the 6th? We can talk details about the C-section then. Just get some rest. You're pregnant with a toddler. This baby might come out walking."

[Water]

In the predawn hours of September 2, I woke to Deana banging on our bedroom wall from the bathroom, yelling at me to get up. "I'm up, I'm up," I said. I knew. She yelled at me to come to the bathroom.

The scene I recall in the bathroom is one of the many, many reasons I get confused by the sentimental cloud that hovers over much of the common discourse on pregnancy. I once wrote an essay, for example, about the birth of our first child, which included a realistic, concrete description of Deana as she began her labor, and I took it to a manuscript critique group. "What is going on?" one reviewer commented on that particular scene. "Shouldn't this be a tender moment? She seems far too grumpy."

Saying that my wife's "water broke" that morning of the 2nd would be a profound understatement. Anything I could say would be an understatement, in fact. This essay is an understatement.

But the spirit of God moved upon the face of those waters, to be sure. The spirit of God moved upon the face of that water there in our bathroom, on the face of the water and the blood, on the face of the child inside my wife, the little girl moving there in the wake of the waters. Breaking water. Flowing spirit. Moans. Contractions.

We called the hospital and went on our way, leaving our son at home, toddling in the living room, holding his blanket, sleep still in his eyes, in the care of his grandmother. "Opal's coming," I told him. "Opal come," he said.

[Waiting]
No room in the inn. Just a hallway. A nurse rolled out a room divider, a blue canvas stretched across a metal frame. "We're growing here at Northside Cherokee," she told us.

Deana labored there in the hall, behind the rolling wall, for nearly three hours. No epidural, either—they couldn't give her that until they took her to the operating room. Passersby looked through the gaps in the temporary wall, hearing Deana's groans, averting their eyes when their eyes caught mine.

It turns out there was also no operating room. The nurses said something about a plumbing issue, water breaking through the ceiling of one of the operating floors, flooding some of the rooms, making them unsuitable for surgery. So Deana continued to labor, waiting, contractions growing closer and closer.

Deana's obstetrician came for us at last and down we went to a recently cleared OR. The doctors wheeled Deana into a room and left me in the hall, in my scrubs, waiting. "Opal come," my son had said, not really knowing what he meant. "Opal come." I'm not sure I knew what those two words meant, either.

Doctors and nurses walked by, congratulating me, asking me how I was doing. One doctor told me she wasn't used to seeing fathers waiting out in the hall to go in the

OR but she was glad I was there. I didn't know whether this meant they usually didn't do C-sections on this floor or whether they did and fathers didn't usually come; but either way, I appreciated her words.

[Seeing]

A doctor opened the door and told me to come in; he gave me a swivel chair and I sat beside Deana. I held her hand, touched her face, tried to let her know I was there without making her more uncomfortable.

We had been through this before, of course. Cannon, our first, had come by C-section, too, though his was not planned. After seven hours of intense labor, on Christmas morning of 2009, the doctors called it a "failure to descend" and so arranged the operation there on the spot. Neither Deana nor I knew what to expect, and so our emotions that morning were of a different kind than those surrounding our daughter's birth on this September morning not quite two years later. We were excited about Opal's arrival, certainly, but we were not quite so worried.

Despite the early challenges—the health concerns for our unborn daughter, the MRI, the surprise labor, the hallway, the long wait for an OR to open up—we both felt a little calmer this second time around. And so I sensed more about the room and the operation itself: The burning smell of laser-cut veins. The surgeon behind the blue curtain who said, "This isn't working." Deana's moans and violent tremors, much more violent than when Cannon was born. Her irrepressible jolts and jerks when the surgeons started tugging on Opal. Her release, like the exhalation of a Pentecost wind, when she heard Opal crying—a sound we had not heard right away when our son first entered the world.

One of the surgeons, Deana's obstetrician, said that we had a little Deana lookalike. Deana smiled and laughed amid her tears and trembling. I asked the doctors if I could see my daughter. They let me, and I kissed Deana's forehead, walked around the curtain, and again noticed the room: the white radiance; the wires and machines; the lights; the spatters of blood on a blue sheet, on the hands of the surgeons, on their surgical masks; the little buckets full of blood and bodily fluids.

And there she was, there in a clear plastic bin, kicking a little, crying a little, gracing me, *this is our daughter*, dove on the Jordan. She took my finger. I touched her dark hair. There were ghosts there, too, a crowd of them; they had followed me in the room before the doctor shut the door, and two came to the front, two smiling old women with curly white hair, who stood behind me, their loose-skinned, warm hands on my back, looking over my shoulder.

"Hey, Opal Mary," I whispered to the newborn girl.

[Night]
Music meant nourishment and encouragement to me when I was growing up, in my adolescent years through high school. I would often go to bed with headphones in my ears playing old R.E.M. but sometimes older, slower songs. Sam Cooke's songs were some of my favorites. This nightly ritual helped me stave off the darkness a little longer so that I could fall asleep.

I remember one night that I was away from home playing Sam Cooke's "Cupid" over and over. I must have been about thirteen at the time, just shortly after the emotional and psychological abuse I endured at home had peaked. I remember crying as I listened to the music. I don't know if this time of my life is what my mother was thinking of when she sent me a text message the day after my daughter was born to tell me she'd been having nightmares about me, but I'd wager it is.

[Cupid]

I held my crying daughter, on her second day in the world, trying to pacify her. I patted her back, rocked her, gently moved her up and down, whispered to her. Nothing worked and she cried on so I tried singing.

I started with old R.E.M., which my son always seemed to like, though I tried to think of songs with some feminine reference. *"She wore bangles, she wore bells on her toes when she jumped like a fish, like a flying fish..."* *"That's the girl of the hour by the water tower's watch..."*

But they did not work. Van Morrison's "Tupelo Honey" did not work. A couple others I tried did not work.

And then I remembered Sam Cooke. *"Cupid, draw back your bow and let your arrow go straight to my Opal's heart for me, nobody but me..."* She stopped crying and looked up, sensing me, aware, if in but the smallest way, of my shadow and my voice. I kept singing and she kept looking. *"Don't know much about history..."* *"A friend of mine told me one early morning..."* *"How I used to ramble, how I used to roam, oh but since I met that Opal of mine, all I do is stay at home..."* *"This little light of mine, I'm gonna let it shine, let it shine, let it shine, to show my love..."*

I realize that singing those particular songs to her probably had nothing to do with the end of her tears. But they had everything to do with the beginning of the end of mine.

[Light]

Out the window, on the roof, against a backdrop of shadowy pines, beneath a congregation of rain clouds, four crows have descended. They caw and chase one another and play tug-o'-war and keep-away—two with an empty plastic bag and the other two with a strip of tar paper they tore from the roof. Here, on this side of the window, Deana breastfeeds Opal.

I take Opal moments later. I lie on my cot, looking out the window through sunflowers in a vase and open blinds at the slate sky swept with clouds and gathering darkness, while my daughter lies on my chest, falls asleep as the sky turns to ink. She smells like cinnamon and milk, this little light in my arms, rising and falling with each breath I take, my chest rising and falling in the peace of her sleep.

Assaying a Garden

> And I have left even more beautiful words twisted among the
> roots, deep down.
>
> —Carl Sandburg,
> "Instructions to Whatever Gardens"

In the late spring, much too late, I decided to put in a garden.

I decided to dig the garden by hand—not so much to be noble or to "go green," but because I don't have a power tiller. I suppose I could have gone out and bought a power tiller: While on a walk with my son one day, I saw two power tillers sitting for sale in someone's yard, in fact. I looked at the tillers, asked how much they were, and, upon hearing they were $65 each, said that I'd think about it and maybe would come back later.

I never went back because I don't know what to look for in purchasing a used power tiller. I don't know what to look for in purchasing a new power tiller, for that matter, and so I decided to save myself the embarrassment of coming off as a man who wants a power tiller but doesn't know a thing about power tillers and to just dig my garden the old-fashioned way.

Already owning a shovel and a pick, I went out and bought a spade fork and did a little research on double-digging, a method for breaking and tilling the ground with hand tools that my grandfather told me about. I even went so far as to watch an online instructional video about double-digging, narrated and demonstrated by a wiry man in a flannel shirt and straw hat who looked like he knew what he was talking about, and it all seemed easy enough.

Thus equipped, and thinking myself prepared, I went out to my backyard to a space in front of my shed and beside my neighbor's chain-link fence—the only spot in the yard not shadowed by water oaks—and started hacking the red clay and busting clods of grass with my pick.

It wasn't long before my neighbor opened his back door to let out his dogs. I've been living here for a year and still these dogs—three little terrier mixes of some sort—always bolt to the fence yipping and snarling whenever they see me, and this time was no exception. The fact that I was swinging a pick and had tools propped against the fence riled them up even more. Then my dog, as she always does, ran to the fence and barked at the neighbor dogs for barking at her owner and encroaching on her territory. Noticing the clamor, my neighbor waved and walked my way, kicking at his dogs as he came.

"Git, Martha!" he yelled at the biggest one.

I stopped working and said hello.

"Getting ready to build something?" he asked.

"No," I said. "Just digging a garden."

"A little late for that, ain't it?" he said. "A garden should be in by now if you're gonna have one."

"I'm more piddling around than anything," I said. "I'll get it done eventually. Maybe it'll be ready by next spring."

He laughed. "Got a tiller?"

"Nah," I said, "thought I'd dig it by hand. Good exercise, I guess, a reason to get out of the house."

"Well, good luck. I'll reach over and steal me some vegetables when it's in. I've got a couple tomato plants myself," he said, gesturing toward a half dozen vines already about chest-high in their cages. "Help yourself when they're ready."

"Sure will," I said.

"Well, I'll let you get back to it. Gonna go have some ice cream." He chuckled as he turned and walked back through his yard, past his flowerbeds and pecan trees and leafy muscadine arbor, his dogs following behind, the hair on their backs still raised.

෴

As it is now, here in the early summer, my "garden"—which I have continued to dig intermittently but have not come close to planting—is nothing more than a patch of exposed red clay, caked and dried in the sunlight, and the half I've yet to dig has grown tall with weeds and grass.

Reactions to this patch of ground have ranged from cordial ridicule to bewilderment. The last time my father-in-law was at my house, he asked, snickering, "Well, Chris, how does your garden grow?"—a joke he'd obviously been thinking about a while. Someone else thought that I was planning to extend my fence across the yard and was therefore digging a ditch to fill with concrete so my dog wouldn't be able to dig under the new section. A friend thought, as we sat around my backyard fire pit drinking beer, that I'd dug a trench to stop a fire if one happened to break out.

෴

One day, while painting my daughter's nursery, I noticed something moving out in the weeds where I'd been digging. I thought nothing of it at first, assuming what I had seen was one of the many chipmunks that burrow in my backyard. The second time I saw it, I was still unable to identify it, so I stepped out on the back porch for a closer look.

I stood for a moment staring at the bramble and noticed it again, a subtle touch of rust and white among the green, barely moving. When a brown thrasher emerged from a hedge and stood beside the creature I'd seen, ushering it deeper into the weeds, I realized it was a fledgling thrasher.

By the time I noticed the young bird, I'd given up on having a garden for the year. The fledgling arrives about the same time each day, midmorning, shepherded into the shadows by its parent. I watch them from my kitchen window. The parent—whose copper eyes burn even this far away—goes off to hunt, returns, and feeds the mottled chick under the weedy cover. Then the thrashers, young and old, hop into the bramble and thin line of trees beyond the backyard fence, between my house and the back alley of a row of shops on Old Highway 41.

"The completely irreligious mind...is the unreal mind, the tense, void, abstracted mind that does not even see the things that grow out of the earth or feel glad about them," writes Thomas Merton. Before I noticed the daily feeding of the fledgling thrasher, I would've said that nothing grows in my garden. I would've said that I busted the ground to get things ready for next spring, or that maybe I'd have tomatoes by October, or some other self-deprecating joke. But I know better than that now, for my garden grows thrashers if nothing else. And I am sure there is much more, things that I can and will never know.

༄

What does this mean now, here in October, no tomatoes, water oak and sweet gum leaves covering the ground? I've lived in this house a year now with my wife and our son, who is approaching two, and not quite two months ago, my wife and I brought our daughter here to the only home she has ever known.

I do not put much stock in land ownership—from a philosophical perspective, I don't understand how a person can "own" a piece of land—but, that said, buying this home and the acre or so surrounding it has stilled something in me, made me more at peace, and I want to try to belong here. Putting in a garden seemed instinctive, along with putting up birdhouses and birdfeeders, as a way to try to belong to this place.

Buying this house and this land made sense to Deana and me. Each month we are now paying far less than half of what we've paid monthly to landlords and apartment complexes over the years. This is a small house, to be sure—just under 900 square feet—and it is about sixty years old, but it needs no major repairs and has given us the opportunity to learn new things.

But most importantly we are learning how to be part of a family and give ourselves fully to a family that we have created. It is quite meaningful to us, especially now that we have children, to know where we are going to be each year, to know that we can sit and watch the leaves falling, to partake in the autumn—like the birds and other animals around here do—as a season of settling down, a season of ripening, rather than as a time of transplantation, of seeking yet another place to rent.

ॐ

"How do we decide where to dream life into existence? On what scrap of this vast planet should we hammer in our stakes and say 'home'? How do we live there with our neighbors? What level of commitment to landscape is acceptable? What lack of awareness is unacceptable?" writes John Lane in *Circling Home*. These questions have been on my mind lately, too. This desire to belong to a place implies responsibility, and it is a difficult responsibility.

It would be much easier to not worry about putting in a garden, for instance. But I am going to maintain the attempt because I never want to live passively here; I have done that for too long in other places. My children are growing here, and they are watching me grow.

Whether I realize it or not, whether they realize it or not, they are always observing me, learning from me, absorbing what I do—especially my son, who is now toddling around and following me everywhere and who even climbed in my lap at one point while I was typing this essay at my desk jammed here in the corner of the living room, but my daughter, too, who just yesterday started reacting to and smiling at the sound of my voice.

I have to try to belong, to set out roots, not only for myself, but for my wife and my children who have taught me that there are things greater than myself, things that make me greater by being a part of a whole. Anything I attempt—whether writing an essay or putting in a garden—is for them and for this place.

And if I fail, brown thrashers will still come to fledge among the clay, among the weeds and bramble, among my shortcomings.

Walking Around Shining

My son, who just turned three, loves R.E.M. Like me, he's especially fond of material from the band's early years. The first R.E.M. song I ever played for him was "Driver 8," from *Fables of the Reconstruction*, thinking he'd appreciate its train references and folksy arrangement. He did. For a couple weeks thereafter, it was all he wanted to hear, though soon he became equally fascinated with a handful of songs from *Murmur* and *Lifes Rich Pageant*. (He might just be the only three-year-old in the world, for instance, who knows all the lyrics to "Swan Swan H," R.E.M.'s strange, haunting take on the Civil War ballad.)

We've only recently gotten to *Out of Time*, which, though nearly twenty-five years old, my son refers to as "the new R.E.M." His captivation with that album started when he heard the melodic opening bass and entrancing vocals in the chorus of "Belong," but it wasn't too long before he became enamored with the track right before it: the infamous "Shiny Happy People." Now every time we get in the car, that's the song he requests. It's his new "Driver 8"—worse, really. At least "Driver 8" is a great song. I've made some desperate reaches for *Green* and *Automatic for the People* because of this, but—while my son appreciates certain moments in both these albums—we can't get past *Out of Time* and the song that Michael Stipe himself has said he hates. It's on a maddening loop, to say the least, both in the CD player and in my head.

Despite the song's irritating saccharinity, which is only amplified by its catchiness, my son's love for it is a grace to my life. My daughter's love for it is, too. In fact, she's the reason I'm writing about it now. She just turned eighteen months old, and so my son's obsession with "Shiny Happy People" has coincided with my daughter's seemingly overnight recognition of music and her comprehension and use of new vocabulary, of phrases that her mother and I didn't deliberately teach her—phrases, incidentally, like "happy people." She's almost always in the car when that song's playing, and she's even started asking for it herself. "Happy people! Happy, happy!" she'll say from her car seat in her newfound toddler voice, and there's really no profound, unsentimental way to describe it: It's pretty much the cutest thing in the world.

She did this in the car the other day, when it was just her and me, and the moment was almost epiphanic. "Happy, happy!" she said as I was getting her out of her car seat, hoisting her over the console and onto my lap. "Happy people!"

꙳

Things have been difficult lately, to say the least. Some old fears have come back to trouble my family and me, and sometimes I feel like they're prevailing. I worry for my children daily. I worry for my wife. I worry for myself. And these specific worries, unassailable as they seem, account for only a small part of the vast worry that afflicts the world, a worry that I try to bear inasmuch as I am able but that of course no person can bear fully.

This worry manifests in depression, yes, but it is not the thing itself. Despite being a stigmatized and misunderstood state, depression may at times be nothing more than a sign that one is awake to—that one cares about, that one *feels*—the greater worry of the world. The worry of the world, which does not recognize the individual human face, pervades the mass and is in fact defined by the mass. Mass incarceration, mass killings, mass warfare, mass ecocide (literally *the killing of home*), mass violence of all kinds: All these things are legion. To try to bear them is to be overrun.

Yet they cannot be ignored, though broken bones come as the price for caring. I've tried to care as much as I can. I hope that my writing is, or at least will be, some evidence of this. I hope that my involvement with organizations like One For Ten, which is working to shed light on the injustices of the death penalty, is evidence of this, too, though I can scarcely read or hear about a death penalty case—such as that of Sabrina Butler, who was on death row over five years before being exonerated in the murder of her nine-month-old son—without feeling physically sick and spiritually impoverished. And the death penalty, of course, is not all. I know that there is no limit to such wounding as the mass can inflict. I care for and I have been broken by much more. Why care at all, then?

I have no perfect answer, but only a sign in the memory of a little girl I dearly and desperately love saying, "Happy, happy people!" in my lap in the car. Knowing no grandiose meanings, she was only mimicking a song which, to her, equates to the sound of the human voice, the words of her brother and the music he loves.

ॐ

This brought to mind Thomas Merton and his "Fourth and Walnut epiphany," a vision he had in Louisville, Kentucky, "in the center of the shopping district," where, in his words, "I was suddenly overwhelmed with the realization that I loved all those people, that they were mine and I theirs, that we could not be alien to one another even though we were total strangers."

Standing at the street corner, he sees separation is a myth, that everyone—*everyone*—belongs to God. Recalling the moment, he writes: "I have the immense joy of being man, a member of a race in which God himself became incarnate. As if the sorrows and stupidities of the human condition could overwhelm me, now I realize what we all are. And if only everybody could realize this! But it cannot be explained. There is no way of telling people they are all walking around shining like the sun." It is hard enough to see that we are all walking around shining when my daughter utters, "Happy, happy people!" against the realization that many people, myself included, are incredibly burdened and sad; it is nearly impossible to see it all the time. Yet we are shining, the beloved and the stranger the same.

There are times my daughter will take me by the hand and everything dissolves into the light of a country I can only by prompting remember, which is the only country she knows.

Interlude, First Movement

MY DAUGHTER LAUGHS IN HER SLEEP

Near midnight, I sit at the computer
waiting for clothes to finish drying,
skimming an article on the *10 proven ways*
I might curb my depression, expecting nothing
but the normal procession of today to tomorrow:
I will fold the clothes, unplug cords,
cut the lights, lock the doors,
resisting the urge to check every closet,
to look beneath the couch, within each cabinet,
any place someone intent on harm might be hiding—
a secret bedtime routine of my childhood.

Over the dryer's thump, heat pumping against
a 20-degree night, wind rushing the vinyl siding,
I hear my daughter react to some vision,
giggle like she does when we play,
two-year-old girl who was not long ago
resisting sleep, as I at times resist waking.

Let me believe in whatever it was she just saw,
in whatever it was that danced through her mind
and she found to be funny, whatever jest,
whatever joy, dwells in her dreams,
whatever it is I so often forget
though it abides in darkness
just the other side of the wall.

Part II: In the Disturbance of Song

The delicate action of grace in the soul is profoundly disturbed by all human violence. Passion, when it is inordinate, does violence to the spirit and its most dangerous violence is that in which we seem to find peace. Violence is not completely fatal until it ceases to disturb us.

—Thomas Merton, *Thoughts in Solitude*

Meditation on a Little Boy Touching His Face

Everything that touches you shall burn you...
> —Thomas Merton,
> *The Seven Storey Mountain*

My child wakes from his nap as early afternoon sun filters through window blinds he bent not long ago. There are times he wakes upset, crying, but not now: Now he grins, laughs when he sees me. Brown eyes. Little teeth. I pick him up, he touches my cheek, says "beard," touches his own cheek and says the same.

"You don't have a beard, goofy," I say. "That's your cheek. *Cheek.*"

"Cheek!" he says. He pats his face, pats mine again, almost a slap. He looks. "Nose," he says, touching my nose. He touches his nose. "Ear," he says, touching his ear. He pulls my ear. "Eye," he says, pointing to his eye. He pokes me in the eye and says "eye" again. "Hair," he says, the last part of the body he names as I carry him out the door.

His fingers touch his wispy hair, his tiny human hand among light brown curly cells.

ৡ

This happened the morning before I first saw *Original Child Bomb*, a documentary on the bombings of Hiroshima and Nagasaki, named after a Thomas Merton poem about the same events: Black and white images. Bodies, babies dissolved into rubble. Children, their faces melted, touching scarred cheeks. No noses. Seared ears, liquid eyes poured out. Hair singed, patches of radiation. Tiny human hands burned by light.

The father of the atomic bomb quotes the *Bhagavad-Gita*: "If the radiance of a thousand suns were to burst at once into the sky, that would be like the splendor of the mighty one."

Others of the Trinity test quote the Gospel: "Lord, I believe. Help thou my unbelief."

Thus they idolize the millstones bound to their necks as a mother who lost her infant in the blast weeps beside a river, her clothing charred to nothing, milk dripping from her breasts. She gives her milk to another child, alive and burned.

It is not hard to imagine that sometime before the bomb fell, a father was holding his little boy, the child, full of new words, touching his face and his father's, saying, in his own language, *cheek, nose, ear, eye, hair.*

Prayer for the Anawim

December 17, 2012

I cracked my children's bedroom doors, looked upon them as they napped, upon two children vulnerable to anything they had mistrusted, which could be anything. Surely sleeping innocents do not belong in such times we call *these times*.

The other day, an image seared my mind like flame to flesh: Another child killed by fire set by bombs, this time in Syria, this time at a makeshift hospital, this time by powers and principalities with no sense of a child's face, filmed in ash, blood-smeared, of a crimson stream tracing the corner of her mouth, an untranslatable word in the tongue of the kingdom of the air.

Yet there they were, my children sleeping, a bit congested, but *breathing*, their tiny lungs rattling whispers, the blankets on their backs rising, falling, almost imperceptibly as prayer.

Into this silence broke a new noise, coursing wires like the last: news of more dead children, this time in this country, this time at an elementary school, this time death sown by a young man pouring bullets into bodies—bodies not much bigger than those taking, releasing breaths beneath blankets down the hall—then into his own. These are the times prayer is not known for what it is. Prayer gathers in my lungs like blood at the corner of a child's mouth, wherever that child fell, whatever her name. Her name is prayer.

My best supplication is a hemorrhage compared to these. I have breathed too much, spoken too much in the corporate tongue. I know nothing but a choked, inadequate language, though yesterday I saw a heron standing on a bridge rail, keeping watch over Pine Mountain Lake, fishing the shallows, its face grave as an evangelist's. My wife and I watched our son and daughter approach it, their feet padding wooden beams.

Our daughter, who had never seen a heron, pointed as she wobbled nearer this bird twice her height, turned to us, made sounds of lost meaning, perhaps asking us to see, though we could not. Finally the heron flew, a feathered jeremiad spread over the lake, its ancient groan echoing something to me like a voice heard in Ramah, blue wings to my daughter's eyes something new as the shekinah light.

Reckoning These Ruins

In the May 1961 entry to "On Pilgrimage," her column published by *The Catholic Worker*, Dorothy Day writes: "So many things are happening in the world and we are brought so close to them by newsprint and radio and television that one feels crushed, submerged by events."

Though I would like to be, and though I try to participate in and speak for just causes as I can, I am no activist in the sense that Day was. I am simply a stay-at-home father and part-time college instructor trying to make a way for my family. Yet I often feel crushed and submerged by the world's events, too, and that has been especially true of late. Thus I have fallen silent.

Perhaps the breakdown occurred between the time Trayvon Martin was killed and his killer acquitted. I spent days and weeks the summer of 2013 following the outcome of the case, reading every article I could, watching every interview I could, and also grieving—even internally raging—over the apparent joy with which many people, the vast majority of them white "Christian" men, welcomed not only the verdict but the death of this young man.

The night the verdict came in, I wept for him again. I wept not so much because his killer had escaped justice—though he had—but because, in the absence of such justice, a young man's death had been justified by the rulers and authorities, the principalities and powers not of some evil, unseen realm, but of this world, this country. I knew, too, that if I had been that young man, or if my son had been that young man, or if any white person had been that young man, the outcome would have been different: He either would not be dead, which seems most likely, or his death would not have been accepted in the eyes of the law. And there would not have been an abundance of white people rejoicing as they danced on his grave.

Shortly after reading and trying to stomach the news that July night, my toddler son, whether awakened by a bad dream or something else, walked into the living room where I was sitting and asked me to lie down with him, which I did until he fell back to sleep.

In Day's column "On Pilgrimage," after cataloging some of the world's events that had been crushing her—the Bay of Pigs crisis, the trial of Adolf Eichmann—Day goes on to quote Martin Luther: "If I knew the world were coming to an end tomorrow, I would still go out and plant my three apple trees today." She connects this outlook to the invaluable service of the Catholic Worker Movement— caring for the sick, feeding the hungry, offering clothing and shelter to those in need, going to jail when necessary— as well as to facing the joys, difficulties, and necessities of daily life.

When I lied down with my son that July night two years ago, that, perhaps, was my way of tending to a seed despite broadcasts of brokenness and all manner of events that pointed to an end—not the sort of end to which fundamentalist preachers constantly point, but the end that bears upon and crushes us now, a nihilistic end in which we care for no one and nothing outside of ourselves.

≫

I am still tending to such seeds. As I write this now, it is an early morning of July 2015. My son is sitting in the living room eating a toaster waffle and reading *Curious George*. My daughter is still in bed but beginning to stir; she woke about an hour ago, asked me for some water and then to cover her up with her blanket, and went back to sleep. Soon, once she's up and ready, we'll all go on a stroller run. Out the window, the bluebirds that have nested in the box by the fence are beginning their daily work of finding food for their young, two chicks that will be fledging any day now. The Cherokee Purple tomatoes I planted with my children back in the spring are ripening on the vine.

In the two years since the night I lay beside my son, the night of the verdict, names have passed like pages in a modern book of Lamentations: Rekia Boyd. Jordan Davis. Renisha McBride. Dontre Hamilton. Eric Garner. John Crawford. Michael Brown. Tamir Rice. Anthony Hill. Eric Harris. Natasha McKenna. Tanisha Anderson. Walter Scott. Freddie Gray. Cynthia Hurd. Susie Jackson. Ethel Lance. Depayne Middleton-Doctor. Tywanza Sanders. Daniel Simmons. Sharonda Coleman-Singleton. Myra Thompson. Clementa Pinckney. So many others, known and unknown. So many other pages. So much more sorrow like this sorrow.

And now we are faced with news of the death of Sandra Bland and the murder of Samuel Dubose. In response to these losses—which are not isolated "tragedies" but the fallouts of a structure that has no regard for black lives—I have nothing to write that has not already been written by people whose insight well surpasses my own, whose lived experience expands well beyond my own. I agree with Roxane Gay, for instance, who writes that even if Sandra Bland did commit suicide—an official narrative to which neither Gay nor I necessarily subscribe—"there is an entire system of injustice whose fingerprints left bruises on her throat." And I agree with Shannon M. Houston who, writing on the deaths of both Ms. Bland and Mr. Dubose, states that "it's clear that we as an American society have forgotten (or never knew how) to properly mourn"—and, further, when she states that the choice for black Americans to mourn does not really exist because they are "presented with far too many bodies at once."

Far too many black lives have been violently disregarded, murderously disregarded, by the white structure. As a white man, I have nothing to add, nothing to write, to make the truth of this any stronger. I can say, however, that I am listening to that truth as so many have expressed it. I can say that I am trying to learn from such listening, to act upon such learning. I can say that I am trying to raise my children in this spirit. I can say, as one who has been absorbed by the structure, as one who has been assumed content to be part of the structure, as one who once was content to be part of the structure because I was unaware of it and didn't need to be aware of it, as one who has benefited from the structure, as one whose silence the structure welcomes and upon whose silence the structure depends, as one who looks like the structure and is expected to carry on the legacy of the structure, as one who could fade into the structure—I can say that this structure is really a ruin.

It is possible to be white and be "crushed, submerged" by such events as these surrounding the deaths of Sandra Bland and Samuel Dubose, the Charleston 9 and Tamir Rice; it is possible to be crushed by the ruin, the amassed pieces of a racist structure that we have too long ignored for what it is. (As Malcolm X notes in his *Autobiography*, "This pattern, this 'system' that the white man created...that system has done the American white man more harm than an invading army would do to him.") It is possible for sincere white silence in light of such events to be a function of being crushed. But being crushed is not complacency, and must not be mistaken for complacency.

I have nothing to say except, by God, let it end. Let us bring it to an end. Let our voices rise from this ruin, against the silence that the structure expects from us, the silence that suggests acceptance and peace at being submerged in wreckage, lying by as this corrupt structure takes more and more lives it regards as nothing—a child in a park, nine people gathered in a sanctuary, a woman who knew her rights and asserted her humanity, a man who spoke and acted in peace, just trying to get home. There is no true peace for anyone here, and I will not be silent.

Of War and the Red-Tailed Hawk

The story of the red-tailed hawk roils with my blood, fused with the dirt at Kennesaw Mountain. Kennesaw rises in the suburbs northwest of Atlanta, an isolated ridge—monandock, "lonely mountain"—in the shadow of which thousands of soldiers fell in a battle of the Civil War, June 1864, one of the last battles before Atlanta itself fell. I fell at Kennesaw Mountain, too, one humid morning in the summer of 2015.

I have not stopped trying to return to that place I fell, to that insignificant spot beside a patch of insignificant wildflowers on a red clay trail between the Dead Angle and Dallas Highway, where I was stroller-jogging with my children just before a hawk walked from the woods.

I have not stopped trying to return, return to the time this place—Kennesaw, *Gahneesah*, "place of the dead"—belonged to the Cherokee; back to the Trail of Tears; back to the battle, the boys, old men, fathers, brothers, sons in blue and gray, many dying for powers that cared not a thing for them; back to the time I first set foot on this terrain, not long after I moved here when I was in middle school and walked these trails with my parents, who were battling through a divorce, and I noticed the prickly pears, the fence lizards, the red moss and blue-gray lichen, everything close to the ground.

༒

I started running again in 2013. My son was three at the time, my daughter one, and, at thirty, pushed by a manifest fear, I'd recently stumbled into one of the worst states of depression I've ever encountered. This depression never leaves; sometimes it's just easier to deal with than others. But late summer 2013 was not one of those times.

I'd grown inactive, downing beer after beer, eating mostly junk, and came within a pound of 230. At 6'1", my healthy weight is around 180, 190 at most. Nearly hitting 230 shook me awake, and I started running—mostly stroller jogs, pushing my children along the way.

On that summer morning nearly two years later, that summer morning of the fall and the hawk, battlefield grass heavy with dew—my son five, my daughter three, myself thirty-two and a good bit lighter than two years before—we were stroller-jogging as usual, only breaking the normal routine of backroads and sidewalks around our house by visiting a trail at Kennesaw Mountain, one I remember running with ease in high school and college.

As the most significant greenspace in the suburbs between Marietta and Kennesaw—one with no parking fee, at that—Kennesaw Mountain National Battlefield Park draws a crowd, and that morning my children and I arrived was no exception. We circled the new lot on Burnt Hickory Road several times, finally found a space as a dog-walker was leaving, and, after a prolonged visit to the Port-a-John at the trailhead—an adventure in its own right—we were on our way. I gave Cannon and Opal each a cup of trail mix to keep them occupied in the stroller, which we call the Flyin' Umbrella, and I took off down Noses Creek Trail, bound for Cheatham Hill and the Dead Angle a couple miles south.

I've always had this rule with running, going back to high school, that once I set a destination in mind, I won't stop, not even to walk, until I make it. Even for the years of inactivity in my late twenties and early thirties, that rule reasserted itself on Noses Creek Trail with my children. Clearly, it was not a rule I formed in a time when I had any idea what it would be like to run a hilly trail pushing 80 pounds of cargo while out of shape. But the rule remained instinct nonetheless. By the time I'd crossed the Noses Creek bridge at a steady clip (the steadiness thanks mostly to the slight downhill grade and the forward momentum of the stroller) and hit the biggest uphill section and obstacle between us and the end of the run, I was grimacing, straining, gasping. Cannon and Opal were spitting raisins from their trail mix at each other. A runner passed us from behind, turned and said "Impressive!" without breaking stride, and continued on her way, soon out of sight.

I never stopped, and we of course made it. It's hard, anyway, to dwell too long on physical exhaustion at a place like Kennesaw Mountain. One hundred fifty years ago, men my age in those same summer woods through which I dashed with a stroller were wearing wool, digging earthworks that still surround the trails, dragging cannons, fixing bayonets, killing each other and trying not to be killed.

In a letter to his wife on June 30, 1864, following the Battle of Kennesaw Mountain, Union General William Tecumseh Sherman wrote, "It is enough to make the whole world start at the awful amount of death and destruction that now stalks abroad. I begin to regard the death and mangling of a couple thousand men as a small affair, a kind of morning dash—and it may be well that we become so hardened."

This passage from Sherman has stayed with me and helped form my understanding of what happened at

Kennesaw Mountain and the manifestations of callousness as virtue that are with us today. While it's true that Sherman probably never imagined an out-of-shape, depressed man in a Kennesaw State ball cap, moisture-wicking shirt, basketball shorts, and running shoes winding around those earthworks while pushing a double-stroller holding two kids spitting raisins at each other, that morning run, my "morning dash," is the kind of small affair he describes—something to get out of the way, over with, nothing too remarkable. A run in the woods, the killing and mangling of people, six in one, half-dozen the other.

The week of my "morning dash," a white supremacist went to Charleston and murdered nine black people in a historic AME church—a present-day act of racial terror of the very same lineage as the 16th Street Baptist Church bombing in Birmingham, 1963, which was of the lineage of Jim Crow, of the so-called Redemption, of the failures of Reconstruction, of the Civil War, of slavery and the Middle Passage.

The mass has accepted that, too. Horrible, but a small affair, it says. There is no other way, nothing to learn from our history, it says. All the NRA decals and Confederate flags that have always been here but in the wake of Charleston have proliferated around Kennesaw, the South, the country, suggest there's nothing we can do, just like the powers and principalities would have us believe there's nothing that could have been done or to be done about any other form of violence. It's all just a morning jog, and only a fool would think otherwise.

᪇

Even a suburb bears mystery—mystery choked by traffic, sprawled and whitewashed and gentrified and homogenized to nearly nothing, chained by the chain stores, boxed by the big box stores, stripped by the strip malls, worn out, disturbed, overrun, mystery seldom heard or sought. But it is here.

Consider the fence lizard, *Sceloporus undulatus*: a copper-plated reptile that, though the longest would only span my wrist to fingertips, recalls the time *Appalachiosaurus* reigned over these hills millions upon millions of years ago. The rushing, scurrying, scratching of the fence lizards among the split-rail fences and monuments at Kennesaw Mountain National Battlefield Park is one of these suburban mysteries one must be humble enough to lie down to see. My children love to follow these sounds, metallic flashes, Cretaceous eyes, in shadows cast by statues of soldiers holding guns.

These guns keep me moving in shadows, too. This is Kennesaw, after all, "place of the dead"—the best guess at the Cherokee appellation for this ridge, a name to which I cannot ascribe enough significance—for Kennesaw, incidentally, the suburban town named for the mountain, is also the place of the gun. Every head of household within the city limits is required by law to own one. It's a symbolic law, sure, not ever enforced that I know of and probably unconstitutional at that. But as is clear—and it should be clear, if it wasn't before, in the wake of Charleston—symbols cast their own kind of shadow. Wander any parking lot or drive the roads around here, and before too long you'll see the law referenced on bumper stickers featuring two revolvers and the phrase *It's the law in Kennesaw!*

ᕫ

During a break from the stroller run, after we'd reached Cheatham Hill, my children had been playing on the footsteps of the Illinois Monument which stands at the crest of the hill and overlooks a field called the Dead Angle, where the heaviest fighting of the Battle of Kennesaw Mountain took place. Union veterans dedicated the Illinois Monument in 1914 on the fiftieth anniversary of the battle, which they lost, to commemorate their comrades' sacrifices. The face of the monument depicts a Union soldier stoically holding a rifle, two women at his side, ushering him to rest in the afterlife.

That morning, after the run, after my kids chased fence lizards for several minutes as I sat on a bench and watched them, my son asked me who the soldier on the monument was. One thing led to another and before I knew it I was trying to explain the causes and effects of the Civil War to a five-year-old. After I gave my answer, which I'm sure was quite rambling, my son thought about it all for a second, looked at the soldier again, and asked me if Civil War soldiers used real guns to fight. I told him they did.

Thus, there at the edge of the Dead Angle, there in the shadow of a bronze soldier, bronze maidens, bronze lizards climbing their feet on the marble monument, there where war loosed fire on the field and forest edges and fallen soldiers burned alive, there by my answer I welcomed my son into the world—world of the fence lizard and summer tanager, of the oxeye daisy and the deer, world of the creek and meadow, world of the monument, world of the Confederate flag, of slavery, of secession, world of the lynch mob and the ladybug, of white supremacy and the wild iris, world of blood and water, world of war and the red-tailed hawk.

I gave Cannon and Opal some water and a snack— bananas, granola bars. We walked the trails around the monument, cool in shadows, among Confederate earthworks, pines and sweet gums, muddy creeks. We passed what was the grave of an unknown Union soldier, now known and interred in Marietta, his former resting place near the Dead Angle marked by small flags, leaves, covered in coins. Horses trotted by, their riders stopping to let my children see and pet the horses. My children are shy, though, inward, and just hid behind me, not out of fear of the horses, but not quite sure what to make of the people on them. The riders went on, and we went on.

Opal stumbled over a root, skinned her knee a little, so I carried her as she sobbed and we looped back toward Cheatham Hill. As I loaded the stroller back up, she picked a few dandelions "for Mommy," she told me, so I packed those up, too, along with some rocks and sticks and leaves she and her brother had both collected and wanted to take home.

I would've been content to walk, but to get the most exercise out of the morning, and to justify the idea for lunch at a meat-and-three on the way back home, I decided to run both ways. The kids were more or less settled in their stroller seats, fiddling around with their leaves and flowers, sometimes fussing at each other for some small slight—a stolen leaf, a leg or arm in the other's space—but nothing out of the ordinary. I stopped to refill their cups of trail mix and soon they were silent and occupied by picking through the raisins and peanuts to find M&M's, and I was off running again.

∽

The red clay trail between the Dead Angle and Dallas Highway is cut through with runnels, threaded by roots. I'd made it nearly a mile before I hit one root in particular, where woods break to meadow and phoebes hunt in high grass flanked by ghost-green replica cannons, where the highway begins to come into view across battlefields.

I've fallen while running a couple times in my life, always alone. There was no thinking about those falls; I was on the ground before I realized what happened. But this wasn't the case that day at Kennesaw Mountain, the day I told my children about war. I'd never fallen while stroller-jogging before and haven't since, but as a safeguard, there is a strap connected to the stroller's frame that I always wrap around my wrist. It was wrapped around my wrist that day, so the forward momentum of the stroller kept me from hitting the ground immediately while giving me time to realize I was going to be hitting the ground before too long. There was no regaining control, no keeping my feet.

After flailing behind the stroller as best I could for three or four seconds that seemed much longer—having lost the handle, held to the stroller only by the safety strap wrapped around my wrist, the world around me a yellow-green blur, my senses anchored only by a blue stroller holding my children, a stroller that would soon be careening and flipping if I didn't let myself fall—I went down. I collided with the trail in a baseball-style slide, the idea being to slow the stroller and stop it if I could, or if it was bound to fall, too, to let it fall back on me rather than trying to keep my feet and risking us all flipping in a tangled mass, crashing into a tree, or my kids being thrown out if it fell forward.

Red clay, rock shards, roots bit into my calves, my thigh, my side. The stroller dragged me forward several feet as I held to the strap wrapped around my wrist. Then the stroller fell backwards, on top of me, and we skidded to a stop at the battlefield's edge. I untangled my leg from the undercarriage and checked on my children, their eyes wide, lying on their backs, feet in the air, covered in M&M's, peanuts, raisins, sunflower seeds, still holding their empty cups. Opal intimated crying and let out a couple forced sobs. I unbuckled them, picked them up, checked on them, and when they realized they were okay, unscathed, and that I was okay save a leg trickling blood, they started laughing, and I did, too. Shaking, thankful, laughing.

I lifted the stroller, gathered the water bottles, keys, snacks, everything that had flown out, and repacked it all. I brushed myself off as best I could and cleaned the blood from my leg with a baby wipe while laughing with the kids as they kept repeating, "You fell, Daddy! You fell!" I loaded them back up, too, and the first thing they asked for was more trail mix, given that what I'd filled their cups with moments before now sprinkled the ground like confetti, pickings for mice and wrens.

I decided it would be best to walk until we crossed back over the highway and made it to the wider, graveled, more stroller-friendly Noses Creek Trail that would lead us back to the Burnt Hickory parking lot and home. Shortly after crossing the highway, just as I was getting ready to start running again, a red-tailed hawk walked from the understory bramble into the middle of the trail, where it stood still and watched us. I stopped the stroller, crouched beside my kids, and we watched it, too.

How many years of creation, evolution, regeneration, between that bird and us? How many years of violence and unlearned lessons will we need? How many more years of mournful songs? A hawk emerged from Civil War earthworks, and we watched in silence.

Soon songbirds began chattering at the hawk, and it lifted from the trail, flew into an old beech tree that burst with colors of fleeing chickadees, titmice, cardinals, goldfinches. In the disturbance of song, the hawk waited on a dead branch.

We continued on our way, and, despite the fall, Cannon wanted to run beside me a little ways, so I let him. We crossed Noses Creek together, and he even put his hand on the stroller, helping me push it, Opal inside, nodding off to sleep.

჻

In my darkness, I remember the hawk. I remember its tail, fan of flame in the understory. In my darkness, I remember the speckled chest, black constellations on white plumage. I remember stopping the stroller, three humans watching the bird walk across the trail. I remember the silence.

In my darkness, I remember my son's questions about the Civil War, whether or not the soldiers used real guns, my answer that they did. But it is too easy, too given to cliché, to consider this moment a loss of innocence. Perhaps it is something gained—a memory of innocence. A gift of that memory from a child not yet in kindergarten, a gift made stronger by his sister beside him, too young to even consider the question in the first place. After all, it would now never occur to me to wonder if Union and Confederate soldiers used real guns to kill each other. I know they did. And I know they used bayonets, too. And rocks and limbs, too. Bare hands, even, there on that very field where my son asked the question. I know all the shooting set fire to parts of the woods and some of the wounded burned alive where they fell. Some of the dead burned, too. I know what happened here, and I know the violence that sparked this violence: the chains and cradle-robbing, the bullwhips and bloodhounds, the never-ending labor and nooses. And I know that such violence persists even now.

But in my darkness I remember the possibility, the potential of original thought, the clarity of vision in my son's question: Somewhere in the human story, in the collective imagination, is the notion—rarely acknowledged, and when it is, only as some absurdity, some fantasy—that the way of violence is constructed, an imposition, an idol, not at all a part of who we are, or at least not who we have to be. There are other verses we can contribute, as Whitman—no stranger to the Civil War's bloodshed—reminds us. Somewhere in this imagination is the notion that soldiers might not use real guns—which of course means that in this imagination there is no definition for soldier aside from human being, and by extension no meaning for war.

I carry the grains of red clay from the fall in my blood. I will always stumble, and I will always remember. In this stumbling and memory, my prayer is that we see a new path and walk it, that we emerge from these confining earthworks, that we find a new story and tell it, that in the disturbance of song, we wait on this dead branch together.

Interlude, Second Movement

AT THE ETOWAH MOUNDS

We enter the ancient village by footbridge,
my son running ahead through a meadow
where butterflies and purple flowers bead the green,
my daughter bound to my hip, chomping a cracker,
crying every time I try to put her down.
A weedeater crops grass at the base of a mound
built by a people whose hush would fill a thousand years
were it not for these hills, the relics of culture
displaced in the wake of DeSoto and disease.

The machine whine stifles midmorning sounds—
birdsong, wind whistling in native grasses
planted by the DNR,
the whisper of the Etowah
making its way to Allatoona Dam.
We take a staircase up the side of Mound A,
rest on a bench at the top for a snack,
share lukewarm water from a plastic bottle.

The temple that once stood where we sit
binds itself now to a thing unknown,
as do the daub huts and cornfields
that filled the river valley
when a priest held this highest place
and two other mounds, almost as high,
housed the dead.

Today the only divination
pours from the coal plant due west in Euharlee,
smokestacks tracing skyline

like an invisible past, a thousand years gone,
still hardly anything figured out.

Tired of the bench and the stillness,
not troubled enough to take in the view,
my children tell me they're ready to go back down,
run the trail by the river, sit in a swing, see the geese.
I pack up the crackers and water,
pick up my daughter, hold my son's hand,
lead them back to lower ground.

Part III: Fragments from Emmaus Road

In affirming my belief in Christ's teaching, I could not help explaining why I do not believe, and consider as mistaken, the Church's doctrine, which is usually called Christianity.

—Leo Tolstoy,
The Kingdom of God Is within You

It is an anonymous and unknown Christ who comes in merciful hiddenness to the distraught pilgrim, as He did to the travelers to Emmaus.

—Thomas Merton,
Conjectures of a Guilty Bystander

Thoreau's Gift

The only faith that men recognize is a creed. But the true creed which we unconsciously live by, and which adopts us rather than we it, is quite different from the written or preached one.

—Henry David Thoreau,
Journal, September 3, 1838

Thomas Merton writes in *Conjectures of a Guilty* Bystander, that Thoreau's wandering idleness "was an incomparable gift and its fruits were blessings that America has never really learned to appreciate." Merton is right, and I find his insight quite meaningful.

Today Thoreau is typically associated with environmentalism, and in Merton's time—the 1960s—Thoreau was perhaps mostly associated with resistance to injustices of all kinds: and these associations are correct. But they alone do not contain the fullness of Thoreau's gift, for Thoreau has yet to be understood, widely understood, in a spiritual context. He has yet to be fully appreciated in a religious sense—particularly in a *Christian* sense.

Despite his place in the American canon, Thoreau is a fringe writer, ever present in the countercultural underground. This is true of about every context one can put him in; it is certainly true the spiritual and religious context. Thoreau is a muse for seekers and relatively free thinkers, and as such he is taken to be quite unorthodox: One story goes that a woman was out laying flowers on Emerson's grave and would not leave any at Thoreau's because he was, as she put it, a "little atheist."

While this view of Thoreau-as-atheist is hardly typical today—most people who write him off now do so because they think he was an antisocial crank, a hypocritical idealist, or some of both—there is still a reason fundamentalists of any sort generally ignore him: Thoreau was not a Christian in the conventional sense of the word.

In his early work, *A Week on the Concord and Merrimack Rivers,* he writes, "It is necessary not to be a Christian to appreciate the beauty and significance of the life of Christ. I know that some will have hard thoughts of me, when they hear their Christ named beside my Buddha, yet I am sure that I am willing they should love their Christ more than my Buddha, for the love is the main thing, and I like him too." And he also writes, "It is remarkable that, notwithstanding the universal favor with which the New Testament is outwardly received, and even the bigotry with which it is defended, there is no hospitality shown to, there is no appreciation of, the order of truth with which it deals." Though he admits to a certain prejudice against it, Thoreau calls the New Testament "invaluable," and qualifies his prejudice, almost in direct anticipation of Gandhi: "It would be a poor story to be prejudiced against the Life of Christ," he writes, "because the book has been edited by Christians."

This is the Thoreau I came to when I was twenty-two and ready to disavow Christianity altogether. And though these remarks on Christianity can easily be taken as negative, they nonetheless resonated with me and helped me to realize that I did not have to shed my Christian label at all—that, in a sense, it would be better to struggle with Christianity than to simply leave it behind.

This was one of Thoreau's many gifts to me, and I realized it was a gift—though a difficult gift—when I first read Thomas Merton not long after reading *Walden* and *A Week on the Concord and Merrimack Rivers.* Merton revealed Thoreau's gift for what it was. And Merton, of course, was a Catholic monk, of the Order of Cistercians of the Strict Observance, which is quite significant. It is significant because Merton, though certainly controversial at times, was profoundly orthodox; there is hardly anybody I know of, except perhaps the most obtuse of fundamentalists, who would try and argue otherwise. Merton was a Christian, and a strong one.

I came to Merton rather sheepishly because of some experiences with institutional Christianity, experiences that made me leery of anything bearing a Christian label. The first book I read by Merton, at the suggestion of a mentor, was the deeply Christian *Thoughts in Solitude.* In the preface of that book, Merton writes:

> The murderous din of our materialism cannot be allowed to silence the independent voices which will never cease to speak: whether they be the voices of Christian Saints, or the voices of Oriental sages like Lao-Tse or the Zen Masters, or the voices of men like Thoreau...It is all very well to insist that man is a 'social animal'—the fact is obvious enough. But that is no justification for making him a mere cog in a totalitarian machine—or in a religious one either.

It struck me as odd, and refreshing, to find a true reflection of Thoreau in the pages of Christian orthodoxy. And, even when not directly named, Thoreau's influence absolutely permeates *Thoughts in Solitude*, as when Merton writes, "Let me seek…the gift of silence, and poverty, and solitude, where everything I touch is turned into prayer: where the sky is my prayer, the birds are my prayer, the wind in the trees is my prayer, for God is all in all." That sentence, written by a Trappist monk, is the very heart of *Walden* and Thoreau's work in general, and it contains the principle by which I try to live.

Call it religion. Call it, above all else, a gift.

ॐ

Sometimes Deana and I will talk about religion, and it usually happens on the road. Once, heading out of town, we got on the subject of Matthew 10, specifically where Jesus says (or at least is quoted as saying), "Anyone who loves their father or mother more than me is not worthy of me; anyone who loves their son or daughter more than me is not worthy of me."

That is a hard verse to rationalize in any way aside from a fundamentalist one. Deana and I—both of us Christians—have said before that we love each other more than we can possibly love Jesus, and there is no question at all that we love our toddler son and unborn daughter more than we love Jesus. If I knew, for instance, as a matter of objective fact, that all the torments of hell await me for saying it, I would still say it: I love my son and my daughter more than I love Christ. And Deana would say it, too.

But does this honest proclamation—I would say *admission* if that didn't imply guilt—make us unworthy of Christ?

I do not believe so, and that is what I was trying to put into words in the car—referencing different verses that support my view, bringing up various theological perspectives, all of my discourse rather garbled. All the while in the back, in his car seat, our eighteen-month-old son was passing the time flipping through a book of animal pictures. He must have turned to the barnyard page, which has a big picture of a cow, because, as I was talking about my interpretation of scripture, our son started mooing loudly and emphatically.

Deana laughed, I laughed, and we stopped talking about whether our understanding of Christianity is legitimate.

༄

I can say that I love Christ, but for many Christians this is inadequate—what they demand is a unquestioning faith, an overconfident faith, forgetting completely that faith is only necessary because confidence has limits. Faith is the simple acknowledgement that there are things we cannot know. But all too many Christians believe that faith is nothing more than an expression of that which is known. Faith, to them, is a fact.

༄

Either I understand Christ in human terms or I do not understand him at all. And I may not understand him. But I will not pretend to understand him if he is more mysterious than that. Love is better than understanding, and silence, sometimes, contains more love than can be understood.

If I claim to know anything, I know it is a pleasant evening and there is a breeze here on the Chattahoochee

River rocks and that herons are nesting in a tulip poplar just off the bank. I know that when one of the herons flew from the poplar I was, for a moment, cast in the shadow of its ancient wings.

༰

The problem of literalism: Is Jesus literally a vine, and are we literally branches? The literalists may never admit it, but the true theology of Christianity is a theology of beauty. It is a theology of metaphor, which is to say of poetry.

Or, if it is literal, it is literal beyond our knowing. One of Thoreau's friends said of him: "I love Henry, but I cannot like him; and as for taking his arm, I should as soon think of taking the arm of an elm-tree." Christ said that we should not be surprised if the world hates us, if it despises us, for our branch-like arms.

༰

At my university, there is a designated "First Amendment Area" adjacent to the campus green. As I was leaving class one day, I noticed it was filled with protestors of sorts exercising their right to free speech (on space that, to me, is quite expensive) by decrying homosexuality and the sexual promiscuity of collegiate youth in general. Some were holding signs that read *HOMO SEX IS SIN* and *BIBLE CLASS 101: YOU DON'T DESERVE HEAVEN*; most wore t-shirts that bore messages like *REPENT OR PERISH*. All were harassing passersby with similar messages as what appeared on their signs and shirts. They were, to say the least, fervent in their beliefs—beliefs that, given the many scriptural references on their props and in their hate speech, are allegedly based on Christian principles. They themselves quite obviously claimed to be Christians.

What is Christianity? I do not know. Beyond not wanting to be categorized with the many bigots who swear by the label, my hesitancy to call myself a Christian is due primarily to my ignorance of what such a label means. And yet it is not dismissible because of my ignorance—the truth is not limited to what I can understand. In fact, the truth often gets distorted by my attempts to understand it, in the root sense of *under-stand*. If someone like me tries to perfectly understand Christianity, it would come crashing to the ground.

In one of my favorite poems, "Manifesto: The Mad Farmer Liberation Front," Wendell Berry writes that we ought to "praise ignorance," because "what man has not encountered, he has not destroyed." Whatever truth Christianity may contain is necessarily endangered, or at least threatened, by our encounters with it. But I know this: If the sign-waving people at my college's free speech area were Christians, I am not one. But if we have not yet fully encountered Christianity, it is still alive and the possibility that we might truly become Christ-like remains.

And I believe Christianity is alive, abiding somewhere away from the madness, hidden and broken.

ॐ

One cannot reject or discredit an overused word by making an appeal to its definition or to one of its synonyms. It is quite popular now for Christians to say that "Christianity is not a religion but a relationship," but this does not take into account they etymology of the word "religion," one of the possible roots being the Latin *religare*, "to bind"—i.e., a bond between people and God (or the gods). A relationship, in other words.

What Christians mean by the distinction, of course, is that their relationship is *different*. They mean that theirs is the *right* relationship. That it is *the* relationship, while all the other mere "religions" offer no connection to God or love whatsoever.

ঌ

"Don't believe everything you read; but trust the discernment of God's word." I read this on a pamphlet, provided to me by a Christian, sometime last year. The pamphlet warned me of the dangers of propaganda and made a strong insinuation that President Obama is the antichrist. The contradiction, of course, is that this pamphleteer wanted me to believe the words on the page all the while telling me not to believe everything I read. And so I took the pamphleteer's advice.

ঌ

I am willing to trust the gospel writers and believe that Christ lived; and I am willing to believe, if he lived, that Christ was who he said he was. But along with this belief— or what might be better called this *desire* to believe—I must also keep in mind that if the gospel writers stretched the truth, or if Christ meant something other than I take him for, then there is really no way that I can know.

❦

In his journal for August 18, 1858, Thoreau asked, as so many others have asked, "What is religion?" Following this question, he penned an answer in one of the most refreshing sentence fragments that I have ever read: "That which is never spoken."

The Wren Whistling in the Garden

The wren either hops on your shoulder or doesn't. What he does—this he is.

—Thomas Merton,
Journal, April 5, 1958 (Holy Saturday)

According to some Christian traditions, the wren, like an avian Judas, betrayed the whereabouts of Christ at Gethsemane with its song, leading to Christ's capture and crucifixion. And years later, some say, a wren whistled in the bush where St. Stephen was hiding from a mob of executioners led by Saul of Tarsus. The story goes that when the executioners heard the wren, they turned their heads toward the noise, saw Stephen in the bush, dragged him out, and stoned him.

ॐ

Christ asked Peter: "Who do you say I am?" Many suppose Peter's answer—that Christ is the Messiah (Mark 8:29)—was a foregone conclusion, and so they adopt the very same response; but that is hardly authentic. "You cannot be a man of faith," writes Thomas Merton, "unless you know how to doubt." And he continues:

> You cannot believe in God unless you are capable of questioning the authority of prejudice, even though that prejudice may seem to be religious. Faith is not blind conformity to prejudice—a 'pre-judgment.' It is a decision, a judgment that is fully and deliberately taken in the light of a truth that cannot be proven. It is not

merely the acceptance of a decision that has been made by somebody else.

After Peter's declaration, Christ tells his disciples not to say a word about what Peter had said. Then not five verses later in Mark's gospel, with hardly any time passing so far as we can tell, Christ calls Peter "Satan."

I do not mean to suggest that Christ called Peter "Satan" because Peter answered that Christ was the Messiah. Christ called Peter "Satan," says Mark, because Peter argued with Christ when Christ predicted his impending death and resurrection. My point is simply to show where self-assured slogans can lead: Many Christians would like to believe they are unshakably correct as the righteous Peter of Mark 8:29 and yet retain the luxury of distancing themselves from the satanic Peter of Mark 8:33.

But that is impossible, for he is one and the same. In disavowing the Peter of Mark 8:33 while mimicking the Peter of Mark 8:29, then, many Christians disavow complexity, nuance, and self-reflection—which is to say they trade Christ for a slogan, and do not affirm the righteousness of Christ so much as their own. They take a caroling wren to be an endorsement of their own punitive virtue when in fact the wren sings because that is what God made it to do. For a lovely song they capture Christ, drag out the saints, drive their nails, cast their stones.

୬

Many mainstream Christians today like to assume the garb of a persecuted minority, and so they will print pictures of the president horned like the beast of Revelation and do and say other such things, trivial or quite serious, to conse-crate their own image. *We are like St. Stephen*, they think, forgetting that Christianity might as well be the state reli-gion in America: Nearly eighty percent of Americans claim that they are Christians.

Certainly, this American Christian majority does not go around literally hunting the unbelievers, doubters, seek-ers, followers of other faiths to torture and kill them. And in fact many Christians are kind to such people and grant them their beliefs. Historically this was not always the case: There is no way to tell how many people Christians have hunted, tortured, and murdered over the past 2,000 years.

Yet there is a certain danger in hiding behind such generality. While it may be easier to pinpoint historical examples of Christian violence, surely it still exists. In March of 2011, for example, a Christian in Philadelphia beat an elderly man to death for allegedly making homo-sexual advances. The Christian killed the man with a sock full of rocks and told authorities that the Bible says gays should be stoned.

These stones, of course, are not always literal: It is by now common knowledge, though not acknowledged enough, that LGBTQ youth are at increased risk of suicide and homelessness as compared to their peers. These facts stem from bullying, family and peer rejection, societal in-tolerance, and so on. Christianity is not to blame for all of this, of course, though placing the entire blame on anything is beside the point. Surely many metaphorical stones are marked with Christ's name, and the fallouts are anything but metaphorical.

‰

Rural east Georgia. We are in a cool July rain, just now easing off, casting the field and forest edges and junk piles in a hazy yellow-green. My dogs are on the porch chewing scrap trim; one sticks her snout down in my glass of water and drinks. White lichen, delicate as a moth wing, embraces a water oak. Raindrops fall from the eaves and drip into pools over a floor of moss.

Above me, just beside one of the chains holding up this porch swing, a nest of paper wasps clings to the ceiling, full of eggs and a few larvae emerging from their hexagonal cells. Some of the mature wasps wait on the ceiling, just off the nest, while others attend to their young. There are about thirty mature wasps in all, each the color of dried blood and about an inch long. They seem to be fairly occupied, following God's command to be fruitful, and do not bother me in the least, or even acknowledge me, though I sit right beneath them.

It is strange to watch these wasps tending to their home, working for their longevity, caring for their young, unaware that inside the house there is talk about spraying them with poison.

The rain stops. Water falls from the trees and clangs on the tin roofs of the sheds and other outbuildings. The dogs leave the porch to chase something they sense in the woods. Thunder rumbles lightly in the distance, and the sun breaks over the little mossy puddles.

༄

The wasps are dead. Patches of gray mucus that used to be eggs and larvae dot the corner of the porch in tiny Stygian pools. Some of the wasps lie among these patches; others remain fixed to the nest, ashen and petrified.

A personal statement of faith: There are dead wasps lying around because, in life, the wasps settled too close to convention backed by power, though they of course knew nothing of the convention or of the power.

ᔐ

Sitting at the edge of a field, just past the boneyard of old farm machinery, where I climbed up in an old combine as best I could for a look around—a place one might expect to see a king snake curled up among the rusted junk spilling from the cab.

The machine is now full of abandoned bird nests, some built on top of each other, in nearly every crevice and cavity there is. In the top of the cab, clinging to the ceiling, I saw two wasp nests, both busy with life. They will be left alone in the ruins of this place, their bodies blending with the rust, in a way their kind could not on the porch just a short walk through the woods.

A storm approaches. Traffic noise from the Fall Line Highway isn't far off. The air hums and whizzes, electric with the noise of insects. Smoke-blue light hems the woods.

ᔐ

Too often the Trinitarian aspect of Christianity, informative and beautiful as it can be, degrades into a lifeless sort of dogma counter to the Trinitarian purpose. The dogmatists do not view the Father, Son, and Holy Ghost as any illus-

105

tration of the interconnectedness of God and all things. They do not see the Trinity as a lovely manifestation of the Christian belief that God cannot be reduced to one persona (or gender, for that matter) or spread thin, as in a Greco-Roman pantheon. Rather, the dogmatists see the Trinity as yet another bulwark of rote, formulaic Christianity. To them there is nothing mysterious about the makeup of the Trinity; it is just another thing to accept and profess.

᰾

An image: The nativity, a holy light shining on the Christ Child and Mary, angels and shepherds and animals attending them in adoration, the weary world rejoicing—in a picture on top of a pump at the gas station, framed in an ad for cigarettes, so it seemed the holy light shone from the surgeon general's warning.

᰾

It is odd that the twin stories of the wren betraying Christ and Stephen would emerge from Celtic Christian culture, a culture that, perhaps more than any other in Christian history, has passed down a heritage of earthly religion, of faith embedded in ecology.

Take, for example, these lines from "The Hermit's Song," a poem attributed to St. Manchan of Offaly, one of Patrick's converts: "I wish, O Son of the living God, O ancient, eternal King, / For a hidden little hut in the wilderness that it may be my dwelling." And the poet continues, "Quite near, a beautiful wood around it on every side, / To nurse many-voiced birds…" The whistling wren, presumably, would be among these many voices.

And so I imagine that there is another, kinder possibility in these myths: Perhaps the song of the wren was the last sound that Christ and Stephen heard before the self-righteous mobs took them away. Perhaps the sound gave them joy and courage.

"The first man who whistled," writes Wendell Berry, "thought he had a wren in his mouth." It is not hard to imagine Christ whistling among the tombs that first Easter, when Mary Magdalene mistook him for a gardener, echoing the wren of Gethsemane, the first real whistle of the human race.

Christ of the Burnt Men

The clanking of fetters and the rattling of chains in the prison, and the pious psalm and solemn prayer in the church, may be heard at the same time.

—Frederick Douglass,
Narrative of the Life of Frederick Douglass,
An American Slave

On the one hand we are called to play the good Samaritan on life's roadside; but that will be only an initial act. One day we must come to see that the whole Jericho road must be transformed so that men and women will not be constantly beaten and robbed as they make their journey on life's highway.

—Martin Luther King, Jr.,
"A Time to Break Silence"

It seems that more Christians would allow their faith to be informed more freely, more naturally, by the one who they purport to believe was God. It seems the namesake of the religion should be taken much more seriously. One can be a Christian today and ignore Christ's words altogether: Some Christians even *teach* this. Christians are more likely to listen to and take seriously and apply to their lives sermons from the pulpits rather than the Sermon on the Mount.

൴

There is a Christian fixation on the cross that approaches fetish and sensationalism, and thereby marginalization, which would be laughable were it not so misleading.

The cross is often the primary focus of Christianity, mostly at the expense of a focus on Christ, to the point that many Christians seem to only value Christ's life insomuch as it was a necessary and unavoidable precursor to his death. Certified and respectable Christians can, if they so wish, practically deny Christ altogether and reject most of his teachings as long as they claim Christ's death. They see the only value of his life in his death, and the only value they see in his death is that it rescues them from life.

ᦇ

Several summers ago, in my early twenties, about the time I started to openly struggle with matters of belief, I worked at a day camp for local children. One day, a youth group visited the camp and led the children in an arts and crafts project. For this project, the children were given Styrofoam crosses—most likely made in China and bought at some kind of Christian resource store—and were assisted in decorating them with markers and glittery cross stickers.

Imagine if Christ would have lived and been executed in our time. Imagine children 2,000 years from now, in a society with more "humane" tools for murder, decorating little Styrofoam electric chairs and Styrofoam needles bought from a craft store with markers and glittery electric chair and needle stickers.

ᦇ

As I was driving down Main Street, I saw a man carrying a cross on the sidewalk. The man wore bright soccer shorts, shoulder pads, and no shirt. He bore the cross on his padded shoulders. At the bottom of the cross, a little wheel was attached to ease the burden.

How can I laugh at him? Many of us, myself included, attach little wheels to the bottoms of the crosses we carry. And there is a greater danger putting metaphorical wheels on metaphorical crosses. At least this man, crazy as he looked, carried *something*.

ॐ

I read some time ago that 850 million people in the world—about one in seven—don't have enough food to eat. And that figure has undoubtedly increased since I read it. I've heard that some Christians pray to God for help finding elaborate houses and cars, and consider it an answered prayer when they get these things.

ॐ

It was Christians who dropped nuclear bombs on Hiroshima and Nagasaki. It was a Christian president who ordered the bombings. It was a Christian government and population that, for the most part, supported, defended, and justified the bombings.

Christian is a label rooted in the word *Christ*. Christ was man who lived two millennia ago who Christians consider God incarnate, a savior who said, among other things, "Let the children come to me, and do not hinder them."

The bombs dropped and blessed by Christians killed infants nursing at their mothers' breasts. The bombs dropped and blessed by Christians instantly turned children to skeletons. The bombs dropped and blessed by Christians melted the faces of the least of these.

ୄ

Christians are those who, to use Thomas Merton's phrase, "know the Christ of the burnt men," who partake in the suffering of the world and who themselves are scarred in their love.

ୄ

While I understand that corporations are by far more responsible for the devastation of imperiled landscapes than individuals, there has yet been no institutionally religious call—at least not one that has broken through—for individual responsibility. There is, as it were, no call for individual *response*, aside from the weekly calls to respond to the Gospel message by walking a church aisle and mutter "a sinner's prayer."

It is hard to think of the pretentiousness of the industrial church without remembering the first lines of an Emily Dickinson poem: "Some keep the Sabbath going to church;/ I keep it staying at home,/ With a bobolink for a chorister,/ And an orchard for a dome." Many churchgoers keep the Sabbath going to air-conditioned churches, full of flashing lights and electrified music, enhanced by Power-Point presentations, televised sermons, and hologram pastors, all made possible by the automatic teller machines in the lobby. We have rightly agreed not to drive bulldozers, power shovels, and augurs into such church buildings, and we have rightly agreed not to rig church buildings with dynamite, no matter what resources lie beneath them; we have agreed not to dump sulfuric acid and other contaminants into church plumbing systems; we have agreed that it is not good to arrest elderly women or shoot young men who are so audacious as to want to defend church property from corporations bent on destruction; we have agreed not to desecrate the coffins of children laid to rest on church property, no matter if their graves are in the way of progress.

I am in good company when I say that this respect for the built church—and now the overzealous respect for the industrial mega-church—ought to extend to the kind of church not made with human hands, the kind in which bobolinks sing praise and "all the trees of the wood rejoice," the kind in which "mountains and hills break forth into singing," the kind in which many good people live and worship.

ᔥ

"The test of observance of Christ's teachings," writes Tolstoy, "is our consciousness of our failure to attain an ideal perfection. The degree to which we draw near this perfection cannot be seen; all we can see is the extent of our deviation."

Acknowledging the extent of our deviation from true Christian principles is utterly repudiated by most modern churches and their adherents. What we need to do, they say, is to claim a "personal relationship" with Christ the Lord and know that he will save us from this wrecked and essentially evil world by admitting us into heaven one day—which is to say that he will save our disembodied souls. In such a formula, there is no room for the responsibility of realizing the degree to which we contribute to the wrecking of the world, and thus deviate from Christ's teachings—for in this formulaic concept of salvation, Christian humans have vested interest in the world's wreckage.

This deviation from Christ's teachings greatly troubled Tolstoy, as it will trouble anyone who seriously considers it. It nearly, if not completely, drove him mad. At the very least, to put it glibly, reading the Gospels ruined Tolstoy's career. One can see this evidenced in a photograph of a very haggard Tolstoy, taken not long before he died alone in a train station, having left behind his family and the riches and comforts of his estate at Yasnaya Polyana, seeking, like John Bunyan's pilgrim, "an inheritance incorruptible, undefiled, and that fadeth not away."

I mention none of this to romanticize Tolstoy or hold him up as a saint. Any serious study of his life will reveal that he was in many ways insufferable and a burden on those closest to him, especially his wife. But to dismiss him is another matter altogether. The truth of his convictions and the courage with which he confronted them are in no way diminished because he was also human.

I mention Tolstoy to suggest the great chasm between his understanding of the Gospels and the way many Christians now understand them. Too often, we use Christianity as a way of justifying our waywardness. There is hardly a Christian today, it seems, who cares to consider the personal crisis that a close reading of the Gospels will create. Adherence to the most widely accepted form of Christianity is more likely to bolster, as opposed to ruin, careers. Popular Christianity is now, and perhaps has always been, a means of advancing in the "way of the world"—which, in reality, is only the way of a violent and exploitative economy.

According to Tolstoy, this sort of economy and Christianity are wholly incompatible, and the nearsighted worship of such an economy appears often as the subject of criticism in his religious essays. And Tolstoy's thesis—though it led him to flee his home in despair and perhaps has led to the same things for others—is, over a century later, more in need of realization than it was when he was forming it: The Gospel of Christ is useless if we see it as a mere pact that separates us from a sinful world rather than as a testament to the fact that our wholeness and sanctity are bound to the wholeness and sanctity of the world and its people.

This is a dangerous thesis and can lead to despair over the extent of our entanglement in violence, in recognition of what we have done to the world's wholeness and to its sanctity. But it need not do so, for the very crisis that creates this despair can also lead to its antithesis—that is, to creativity.

Rooted in Her Body

I swear I will never again mention love or death inside a
    house,
And I swear I will never translate myself at all, only to him or
    her who privately stays with me in the open air.
                 —Walt Whitman, "Song of Myself"

The most vocal Christians tend to put Christianity before
our humanity, and so we fail to see how Christianity might
instead complement our humanity—make us more human,
not less.

                      ᴄᴓ

To those who believe in the apocalypse as purification, in
end of times theology—whether they believe the rapture
can be predicted or whether they are like many Christians
who accept that the rapture could happen any minute—I
would suggest spending an afternoon in the woods and
fields with a little boy, catching anoles, finding snakeskins
and pinecones, watching birds, and then, at night, taking
him out to look up at the sky and teaching him the word
"stars." That should cure any talk of a better world.

                      ᴄᴓ

Driving through the mountains with my little brother many
years ago, on our way home from a hiking trip, we came
upon a little white church and a graveyard. My brother saw
the graveyard and asked, "Why do people have to die?" A

sign out in front of the church read: "God has all the answers to your questions."

৵

I was born to Christianity. My parents are Christians, as are my grandparents, as were my great- and great-great grandparents, as in all likelihood were my forbears who went before them. I no more "chose" to be a Christian at a Billy Graham Crusade in 1996 (or the several other times I was "saved"), as I once thought I did, than I "chose" to be a Southerner or an American. It is in my blood.

Christianity, for me, is more of an inheritance than a choice. My refusal to abandon it has more to do with my desire to honor that inheritance than to build walls around myself by staking claims to a "personal" faith. Such an inheritance, of course, comes with scars—as does my inheritance as a Southerner and an American. But such scars, I think, are more opportunities for creativity than for a stale choice between unquestioning acceptance and renunciation. Such an inheritance implies responsibility; it is not a talent to bury in the ground.

None of this is to say that renouncing one's religious inheritance, whether to convert to another religion or to claim no religion at all, does not sometimes have a place in individual circumstances, and as such I can only speak for mine. Even if I were to follow Buddhism, which I've thought of doing, and even if I were to claim no religious label at all, which I've also thought of doing, I would still see Christ playing in ten thousand places, "lovely in limbs, lovely in eyes not his."

৯৹

The odd pairing of hyper-individualism with group think has created a climate in the collective church in which it is deemed honorable to forswear one's family and one's history for the sake of Christ. By this, I do not only mean the joy at which many Christians welcome proselytized "converts" from other perfectly fine religious traditions into the fold; I also mean the kind of snobbish disdain that some Christians have for kindred or communal faith, Christian or otherwise.

To say that "Christianity is in my blood" is not the sort of confession these Christians demand. To them, valid Christian confessions are invariably personal in a strangely public sort of way; they value an imposed sort of personal relationship, as opposed to an inherited one that is shared by family and community and enriched by memory—not beyond criticism or doubt, certainly, but upheld more by loyalty and familiarity than by dogma.

This is why so many "testimonies" of newly converted Christians, especially young Christians, will contain variations on the phrase, "I was raised in a Christian home, but...," usually ending with some statement as to how the convert overcame his inheritance and really "chose" Christ, a Christ supposedly more "alive" and "relevant" in the casual, energetic, and rock-music-accompanied worship of contemporary churches than in the worship of old timers in their supposed dead churches, let alone in the thoughts of a person sitting quietly in the woods.

৯৹

I remember a red clay road out near the Fall Line, sand and decomposing matter at its edge, scat of the night animals, and a gathering of orange butterflies there feeding, unfurling their proboscises into the mineral-rich earth. I remember my son saying *butterfly*, looking at the creatures so intently, so curiously. I remember reaching down by the side of the road, there by the ditch full of weeds and beer cans and crossed by barbed wire—reaching down to let one of the butterflies crawl onto my finger. I held it up to my son, and he watched. To have known what churned in his mind.

The butterfly, like a little flame, took flight, and my son said, "Hold that butterfly again." I let another one crawl on my hand, my soon looking at me, a bearer of winged wildfire in his imagination.

Knowing my son sees me for what I am. Knowing he sees the insects for what they are. *All things counter, original, spare strange.* This is our praise.

᳕

At Our Lady of the Holy Spirit Monastery in Conyers, Georgia, there is a renovated barn. Monks once lived and worshipped in this barn, but now it is part of the monastery's heritage center.

I walked the monastery's prayer path outside the center, where barn swallows were alighting on the power lines, flying away, and returning, their orange-cream breasts and blue-black wings radiant in the sun.

On a sweet gum tree, a sign read: *Sweet gum.* I imagine a monk put the sign there so people would know.

Christianity is curiosity. The arms of the elderly monks are like the limbs of this sweet gum, the body of

Christ like the trunk. *Christ-like* the trunk. Trees are
Christ-like.

&

I stopped at Arabia Mountain, a granite monandock, after
visiting Our Lady of the Holy Spirit. The place is like a
moonscape, almost alien climbing out of the pine forests.
Almost. A closer look reveals it is not alien at all.

This is a place of blending, of oneness, of silence. Little flowers dwell in the shadows of immense metamorphic
and igneous outcroppings. Yellow pistils of lavender meadow beauties reach out like tongues of fire.

Small depressions in the granite, called solution pits,
pock the sides of Arabia. These places are filled with mosses, lichens, grasses, diamorpha—greens, yellows, and reds
cloistered from the burning gray rock.

Desert hermits could live here. Christ could walk here,
and does. I turn to go back to the car, headed home. A lone
cedar trembles in the warm breeze blowing over the barren
rock. The breeze stops. The tree is still but for the movement of a mockingbird.

&

At the monastery, in front of the abbey church, a sculpture
of Mary holding the Christ Child rested over a bed of
white begonias. I stood before it, looking. It reminded me
of the way my wife holds our son, and I imagine her holding our daughter just the same.

My Mary, my Christs. I can believe in that. I can believe in my wife and the children she holds. She holds them

and they belong, rooted in her body like begonias in the garden, like the feet of the Holy Ghost in the earth.

Cadence

MY CHILDREN PILE STICKS ON A HEADSTONE

Before the barbecue, the field peas and cobbler,
before the reunion beneath the shelter,
we must endure revival, or wait outside for the sermon to end.
Every so often, the breeze eases enough that I can hear
the preacher droning inside Antioch Baptist,
a relic nearly overcome by woods off Duck Roost Road,
its windows smashed by vandals, white paint flaked, fading,
this the only day of the year it holds a congregation of any-
    thing
besides mice and wrens, paper wasps, surely occasional snakes.

Every so often, a stare cuts my direction through a broken
    pane;
every so often, the sad discussion of sin and death reaches
the cemetery, over a century old, where I sit with my children
as they gather sticks, start piling them on a headstone.

I stand, tell them *No, no, we can't put these here*, as I move the
    sticks,
my son waiting by the grave with more in his arms,
my daughter collecting those I've tossed aside,
ready to return them to the top of the stone.
At four and two, they don't know what this headstone means,
let alone what death is at all, and intend no disrespect,
despite looks shot through rock-shattered windows,
judgment trailing the sermon's echoes.

I brush the last of the sticks off the grave,
usher my children to the edge of the woods
where they touch moss, part muscadine vines,

draw pictures in the clay sand with sticks
they've carried from the cemetery.
Cicada song settles here, so thick
it drowns the last words of the sermon,
covers every word out of reach of this closeness.
I know nothing of nothingness, either,
here, amid all this.

Appendix

Go to the Ground:
An Interview with Christopher Martin

Author's note: The following interview, conducted by Poe-cology editor Kristi Moos over e-mail between June 2014 and June 2015, was published in the summer 2015 issue of Poecology *[www.poecology.org]. I wrestled with the idea of including an interview in a debut book, but it complements and extends upon the thematic content of this book so well that it seemed to me a natural piece to incorporate. Further, it speaks to the inter-connectedness of supposed dichotomies—poetry and prose, social justice and personal story, narrative and fragmentation, faith and doubt, spirituality and physicality, and so on—that I have tried to speak to in all that has preceded this appendix. It is, at the very least, an artifact from a moment in time, like each piece in this collection, that I have found meaningful and worth re-counting in the hope that readers might take something from it.*

[*Poecology*] Tell me about what the project of poetry holds for you as an ecopoet, an editor, teacher, and reader. What do you listen for when you're out in the world? Has your "listening" changed over time? How does this listening manifest itself, for example, in [your poetry chapbook] *Everything Turns Away?*

[CM] Yes, my listening has changed over time, very much so. So much of being a poet, for me, has been about re-claiming the child-mind, some childlike sense of wonder, that I brushed aside—never completely abandoned, but certainly neglected—somewhere along the way. Learning to listen closely has been part of that reclamation. Spending time with my kids has taught me a new way of listening to the world, of *sensing* the world, too, which in turn has influenced my writing.

Janisse Ray uses this great epigraph to open her memoir *Ecology of a Cracker Childhood*, a line from a poem by Iain Chrichton Smith: "Words rise out of the country." I guess that's part of what I'm trying to get at, as well, perhaps especially with my two most recent chapbooks—this idea that though their terrain is squarely in the suburbs, words rise out of Acworth and Kennesaw, too, whether anyone hears them or not, however much concrete and however many mini-mansions are piled on top of them.

Your question made me realize the sonic quality that weaves through *Everything Turns Away*, which I suppose is a function of the generally untranslatable words that are here if someone will listen. There's a poem in there about a hawk resting on the cross of the First Baptist Church and eventually flying from that cross "by such wisdom / as I do not have, its call trailing / trees in a tongue I do not know." There's another where I basically strip down and follow a kingfisher's cry—also rendered as "laughter"—into a lake cove. There are a couple in there about silence, which of course is its own kind of sound—"My Son Points to a Confederate Flag and Asks What It Is" and "At the Periodic Table Display" (which I'm now calling "My Daughter Touches the Plutonium Square") are examples of this kind of charged silence. There are other "sound" poems in there, too—I guess "The Wish to Sing with Primitive Baptists" is another about imagined sound, a desire for communal sound, sound that ultimately might not be possible but is nonetheless beautiful. There's one about a dead coyote on the shoulder of an I-75 exit ramp that makes me think of this theme of sound in context of these lines from Wendell Berry: "Listen to carrion—put your ear / close, and hear the faint chattering / of the songs that are to come." A few others in *Everything Turns Away* (or maybe all of them) are about sound, about listening, in some way. There's also the epigraph from R.E.M.'s "Texarkana," and I guess the title of the book owes as much to Ecclesiastes, Pete Seeger, and The Byrds—"to everything there is a season," "turn, turn, turn," and all that—as it does to Auden and Breughel.

Beyond that, there might not be anything more important to the progress of humanity than learning how to truly listen to one another. Listening is extremely undervalued thing in the mass culture, though—in the structural culture—so I guess some of my work is about reclaiming the art of listening, holding it as thing of great worth, though of course I often fall short of that.

[*Poecology*] That's really interesting. Can you give an example?

[CM] Take what's happening now with the debate over the Confederate flag: A white supremacist goes to Charleston and murders nine black people in a historic AME church—a present-day act of racial terror of the very same lineage as the 16th Street Baptist Church bombing in Birmingham, 1963, to give just one example. Many black people, and many empathetic people of all races, point to that Confederate flag flying in Columbia and say it's a symbol that causes pain and that has historically caused pain, and that maybe it's time to take it down. Some people listen to that pain and try to respond appropriately and constructively. But then before you know it, you've got rushes to stock up on Confederate flags and memorabilia, parades of trucks flying Confederate flags down the highway, planned KKK rallies, and so on. That an expression of pain on the part of black people could lead to everything from a KKK rally to an individual who imagines himself bereaved unfurling a Confederate flag over his porch rail, that the loss of black lives has in certain respects come to be overshadowed by the overdue loss of a symbol, is a profound failure of collective listening.

You specifically asked about listening in the context of being an ecopoet, so I'd like to explicitly link what I just said about the failure of collective listening—as related to the Confederate flag, racism, racial terror, etc.—to ecopoetics. And to make that connection I want to turn to Natasha Trethewey—not only a poet I admire, but someone I regard more along the lines of a hero.

A couple years ago, I had the honor of assisting my friend William Wright conduct an interview with Natasha Trethewey for the *Atlanta Review*. In that interview, Will asked a question about the theme of nature in poetry, specifically Southern poetry, and this was Natasha's response (which I've only slightly redacted):

> I think of the poet Camille Dungy, who edited a volume of poetry called *Black Nature* in which she brings together all these black poets who deal with nature in some form. She uses as an epigraph some lines from Lucille Clifton, a few of which are 'but whenever i begin / 'the trees wave their knotted branches / and...' why / is there under that poem always / an other poem?' The implica-

tion here is that when she begins to think about trees in a landscape, it's impossible to stop thinking about the violence of the landscape, the lynching. So I think that the landscape for Southerners—both white and black—is steeped in the violence of the past.

This is true of my own perceptions; it's hard for me to escape this idea. I can't walk around my Mississippi, for example, and not think of all the people erased from the landscape. How we have so many places—places that reflect Native American history in their very names—that have for the most part vanished, been bulldozed over [...]

So I think that's why we as Southerners, and indeed, likely poets in all parts of the world, focus on nature as a motif—at least often why we do so: because under our feet lie the remains of another people, another time, a record that informs us.

The landscape also has these manmade additions on top of it, so the palimpsest of a body hanging in a tree is part of the manmade landscape we've created. I think there is a need in our literature to make sense of the distance between those two things, what I call the terrible beauty of my Mississippi—the beautiful natural world there and the palimpsest on top of it.

I don't want to be prescriptive, but I don't think anyone interested in ecopoetics or who writes ecopoetry can stay true to any sense of *oikos*, any sense of home, without acknowledging these ecologies of violence, or, as Natasha Trethewey says, without trying to make sense of the distance between beauty and violence. Kennesaw Mountain and the Allatoona region, for example, are beautiful places. The whole Georgia piedmont is a beautiful place, to get right down to it. But there's also this malevolent palimpsest right on top of it all that can't be ignored if achieving some sense of wholeness for this place and everybody and every-thing in it is the goal. *Poecology* readers might be interested in "What Hangs on Trees," an essay by Glenis Redmond published in *Orion Magazine* a few years back, for more on this kind of thing. I believe it's immeasurably important to think about, to talk about, to listen to each other about.

[*Poecology*] Can you talk more about how teaching, editing, and listening work together?

[CM] As a new teacher, I try to nurture a space for that kind of listening to happen. For example, in one of my classes last semester, we got on the subject of the Civil War in a discussion about Walt Whitman's poetry. The Civil War was a subject that many students in the class resisted, and when I pressed them on why, one student, capturing the feeling of many students in the class, said that thinking about that war and why the South fought it often leads to shame. I allowed the necessary space for that emotion to settle, then we acknowledged it and talked about it. For a few classes thereafter, we focused heavily on Natasha Trethewey's work. Her work, which requires deep, medita-tive listening, provided an entry point to discussing the Civil War. By the end of the semester, for some students, that shame had started to turn to knowledge and under-standing, which for some led to creativity, which I believe can lead to change and to healing.

It's kind of the same thing that guides my editing of *Flycatcher*—I guess I'm just trying to nurture some sort of literary space where listening can happen. The current issue is dedicated to Charleston, for example, and is filled with work that has creatively emerged from similar moments and climates and histories of violence, strife, and discord. I would like to think that poems like Imani Marshall-Stephen's "How Do I Fight?," J. Drew Lanham's "Because of Black Hands," Charlie Bondhus's "Box," to name only a few, would if but for a moment still anyone's urge to immediately respond. The poem is the antithesis to the soundbite, a way to true listening, which leads to empathy.

Holly Haworth has a great poem in the issue that ends with the lines "I have grown / aged here listening," which really could be an epigraph for *Flycatcher* itself and for what I hope to do as an editor.

[*Poecology*] *Marcescence: Poems from Gahneesah*, co-written with David King, explores Kennesaw Mountain in the suburbs of Atlanta. It's a place-based collection that is generous in its contributions to place, and is responsive to the history and people of that place. One of the epigraphs to *Marcescence* comes from Walter Clark, a sergeant in the Battle of Kennesaw Mountain, who writes: "Standing beside the breastworks on that summer evening, under the shadow of grim and silent Kennesaw, with twilight deepening into night, there were shadows on all our hearts as well, shadows that stretched beyond us and fell on hearts and hearthstones far away, shadows that rest there still and never will be lifted." There's a strong legacy of these sentiments in poems such as "Deer Crossing Old Mountain Road," "Battle Hymn: Highway 41, South," and others.

Here, I read an homage to the history and stories of the place, into which you weave strands of personal experience, and into which I read a yearning to preserve meaning while also making new meanings. In what ways do you see

this collection revisiting Clark's idea of "shadows"? In what
ways do these poems attempt to "lift" these shadows?

[CM] Since so many of the poems in the book reference
the Civil War battle fought at Kennesaw Mountain, it was
very important to David and me that one of our epigraphs
come from a soldier who was there. David and I are Southerners; we've both lived in Georgia all our lives. Much of
our work is about grappling with what that "Southerner"
label means and all the burdens it carries. So, as not to shy
away from that, we wanted the epigraph to come from a
Confederate soldier, specifically one from Georgia. After
several months of poring over all the books on the Battle of
Kennesaw Mountain and the Atlanta Campaign I could
find, looking for primary accounts of soldiers who fought
there, those words from Walter Clark stood out as being
quite complementary to—even synchronous with—the
tone of our book. Most if not all of the poems in the book
were done by the time I found that passage.

Walter Clark was an Orderly Sergeant in the 26th
Georgia Infantry. His words in our epigraph are from a
journal entry he made on June 29, 1864, two days after the
worst of the fighting at Kennesaw, reflecting on roll call the
night of June 27. Before he wrote about those shadows falling "on hearts and hearthstones far away," he wrote about
how "the voices of twenty-two of those who had so
promptly answered the call of duty a few hours before were
hushed and silent when their names were called."

So one way this collection revisits Clark's words is in
its attempts to speak for those "hushed and silent" voices,
because in the full context of what Clark was saying, his
metaphorical shadows were a result of silence.

But "speak for" is a bad way of putting it. I don't want to and can't presume to speak for anybody else, not even for ghosts, so maybe it's better to say this collection attempts to turn down the noise and open the doors and windows to better hear those hushed voices. Whether the collection is successful in that regard is up to readers, of course. But the truth is that ignorance of history and the silence that surrounds it are pretty big problems around here. Hardly anybody here seems to understand or even feel the gravity of the Civil War, which I know might sound strange given that this is one of the most so-called "conservative" parts of the country where Confederate imagery and allusions are commonplace and the Civil War is still being fought in many people's hearts and minds. But the true gravity of the Civil War is lost in the mythology that surrounds it, in the way people romanticize it. Even calling it "the Civil War" can be controversial around here, where plenty of people think of it as "the War between the States" or, worse, "the War of Northern Aggression."

I suppose David and I, in our own ways, were trying to cultivate some sense of the Civil War's gravity with this book. No romanticizing it, but no ignoring it, either. Romance and ignorance are probably the two biggest metaphorical shadows this collection revisits, at least in the negative implications of that metaphor, and they are two of the big ones we are trying to lift. You see romance in everything from Confederate flag imagery to the untenable yet strangely popular notion that slavery was not one of the Civil War's causes.

Several weeks ago, in the wake of Charleston, as debates about removing the Confederate flag from the South Carolina capitol and other government structures were taking place throughout the South, and as debates about the very meaning of that flag were taking place here and across the country, I saw shoppers walking out of Wildman's Civil War Surplus and Herb Shop in downtown Kennesaw with bagsful of little Confederate flags, showing their support for a symbol that needs to go. I don't think it's any happenstance that Wildman's dilapidated crypt of a store, one of the places around here where folks seem to be stocking up on Confederate battle flags and other such merchandise, has a noose-wielding Klansman mannequin in the middle of it.

I suppose that could be a metaphor for this whole area: there's a moldering-robe-wearing, battle-flag-waving specter in the collective heart of this place that hardly anybody is willing to acknowledge. Thus the flags, the romance, the ignorance, the misinterpretations—which, incidentally, do nothing to bolster anyone's understanding of or respect for the common Confederate soldier, much less for the causes and effects of the Civil War, less still for those who suffered through it. I doubt any of the folks waving that flag and talking about heritage could tell you about Fort Pillow, for example.

So yeah, I guess that's one of the shadows David and I were trying to lift with these poems, and to do that, to attempt to do that, we had to go to ground in the heart of *Gahneesah*—which I don't think I've yet mentioned comes from an Anglicized form of the Cherokee name for Kennesaw Mountain, and means something along the lines of "burial ground" or "place of the dead." Not to overstate our significance, but the process of daydreaming about these poems and eventually writing them was something like going on a Dantean pilgrimage in our own backyards. There are shadows everywhere here—some a refuge, some more like a shroud.

[*Poecology*] One of the things I admire about your voice is the caring fearlessness with which you balance a critique of contemporary American culture with a religious respect for its iconic places and traditions. It's a tension that comes out so naturally in your work and expresses a certain need to revisit and mull over connections between place and spirituality. If I can quote from the first nine lines of the poem "Feeding American Bison at the Yellow River Game Ranch," from your unpublished full-length [poetry] collection, *All Formations, All Creatures*. Here this tightly woven tension and beauty unravel in a way that uncontrollably hooks me:

> I held my son by his legs, making sure he was secure
> on my shoulders as we looked through the fence at bison
> abiding in the sludge on the banks of the Yellow River.
> Remembering Job and how the Lord spoke to him, saying,
> *Behold now Behemoth which I made with thee; he is chief*
> *of the ways of God, and only his maker can approach him,*
> I watched a bison draw near through tires and hay bales,
> its great head rocking over black earth, the air reeking
> of Kentucky Fried Chicken, chicken shit, and smoke.

Can you give some insight on how you write with an eye for this tension between reverence and irreverence?

[CM] This is another incredible question, and I thank you for what you say in introducing it. Reverence tangled with irreverence—there's evidence of it everywhere, right?

You see this tangling of reverence and irreverence here in a region often called the "Bible Belt" for example. Take the story of Mary Turner, which I only recently learned. In 1918, at twenty-one years old and eight months pregnant, Mary Turner and her unborn child were murdered by a lynch mob outside Valdosta, Georgia. Anyone interested in more information can find it [online] at the Mary Turner Project, and *Poecology* readers might be particularly interested in Derrick Jensen's account in his book *The Culture of Make Believe*. I mention her name here for two reasons: (1) Hardly anyone knows about Mary Turner—or much about the history of lynching itself, for that matter. And it wasn't until 2010 that a state historical marker was placed at the site where she was murdered. (2) If something like this, and this is only one example, could happen in a place that many people have believed and still believe to be particularly holy—the so-called "Bible Belt," as I said—and if people here and anywhere such things have occurred continue upholding myths about godliness rather than grappling with the real story, the real history, then I don't put too much faith in whatever it is we supposedly revere. Reverence and irreverence thus become so entangled that it's nearly impossible to distinguish one from the other.

I'm thinking here of the lines from William Blake:

And did those feet in ancient time
Walk upon England's mountains green:
And was the holy Lamb of God,
On England's pleasant pastures seen!
And did the Countenance Divine,
Shine forth upon our clouded hills?
And was Jerusalem builded here,
Among these dark Satanic Mills?

Speaking of Blake, and back to that bison: Aside from the trip to the Yellow River Game Ranch the poem describes, my poem was inspired in part by Blake's "Behemoth and Leviathan," from his *Illustrations of the Book of Job*. In Blake's rendering, behemoth seemed to me in many ways to resemble a bison.

Of course, behemoth, as it appears in Job and in Blake's rendering, is not literally an American bison; but behemoth, like leviathan, can be taken to be a composite creature, a sort of synecdoche, and in that respect the bison is exactly the kind of megafauna that behemoth could be.

So along with this ancient, scriptural, sacred imagery connecting behemoth to the bison, you've got this creature, the bison, quite iconic in its own right, a symbol for the American ideal right up there with the bald eagle. And yet there an individual bison was, living in a crowded pen full of sludge and shit in the middle of the suburbs. Layer all this with the historical abuse and near extermination of the bison as a species, and you're back to that insurmountable tension between reverence and irreverence.

Wendell Berry has a poem with the lines "There are no unsacred places; / there are only sacred places / and desecrated places." This difficult truth is always on my mind, and I think it gets to the heart of your question and of what I'm trying to say. Where there is desecration, where there is irreverence, there is always a remnant of the sacred, of something worth revering. Sometimes these remnants can be numinous, elusive, but generally I think they're plain enough to anyone who is awake.

[*Poecology*] Your children make an appearance in a number of your poems. How has fatherhood changed your view on writing, and particularly environmental writing?

[CM] Well, for one, I've typed out some of these answers with cartoons playing in the background! And there's the constant up-and-down, back-and-forth that comes with being a parent. At the moment, I'm sitting at the end of the hall by my kids' room, typing while waiting for them to go to sleep. Uninterrupted writing time is hard to come by, as is the solitude that generates good writing. So in that regard, fatherhood changed the view I might've held at some point that the writing vocation is some precious thing that answers to nothing but itself. I was listening to an interview the other day where Shelby Foote was talking about Faulkner, and said something about how Faulkner wouldn't let anyone within twenty feet of him while he was writing. If that were my policy, I'd never be able to write a word, and I know I'm not the only one for whom that's true.

And yet, while dismantling whatever idealized view of writing I might've once had, fatherhood helped me to personally understand the lasting significance of the writing vocation. It's a vocation that can easily lead to self-aggrandizing on the one extreme and self-loathing on the other, and each writer has to figure out how to avoid those extremes in order to do good work. The ways we learn to avoid them are many and varied, and fatherhood has certainly been one of my teachers. In this household's economy, for example, the immediate worth of finishing a poem is less than the immediate worth of any number of things, from breaking up fights to handing out Band-Aids to making peanut butter and jelly sandwiches. But that doesn't mean that finishing a poem isn't worth something.

But to get more at the heart of your question: Fatherhood has strengthened my sense of empathy and has made me think—forced me to think, really—on a generational scale, generational in terms of both past and future. I feel I should emphasize here that this is all just personal, probably even a result of my own weakness and limited vision. Too often, being a parent is presented as the end-all, be-all of human existence, which is a cliché, and a potentially harmful one at that. So I'm not going to be prescriptive or claim that being a parent has given me some sort of special vision unavailable to anyone else by other means. But fatherhood has helped me do good work and leave things better than I found them, and also to understand when I fall short of that.

I'm often characterized as this "Southern narrative poet" simply because I'm from the South and write mostly about actual moments in time in the first person, but I do write to effect change, and I do so thinking more about what my children will have to endure rather than what I will have to endure, though there's of course no telling what we'll have to endure together. And my love for them makes me more constantly aware of my love for other people. All that has lately informed my view of writing. There's so much at stake, and we have to leave something good. Fatherhood helped me see that more clearly, and writing—whether it's about social justice or the environment or a simple moment with my kids or whatever else—is my way of expressing it.

[*Poecology*] Rick Bass said that "all writing is about loss or the recognition of impending loss." The poems in *Everything Turns Away* echo and expand upon this notion—these works never leave us with a simple sense of loss, but also a poetic longing for connection that transcends mourning and sadness. Can you talk more about how loss figures into your work?

[CM] This is a great question, not least because it made me realize that loss is one of the most persistent themes of my writing. And you're right that the poems in *Everything Turns Away* engage this theme directly. I see now that loss was there all along, guiding the book to what it would become. It emerges in just about every aspect of the book— the title, the content of the poems themselves, the epigraphs, the allusions to Icarus, and so on.

I suppose loss figures into my work and this particular book so strongly because of what you say about that longing for connection. I've lived in the Acworth, Georgia, area—which more or less constitutes the geography of *Everything Turns Away*—for many years now. About four years with my family (by which I mean my wife and our two kids), and probably about ten years, not all of them successive, from high school to the point where my wife and I bought a little house here after living a while in Smyrna, which isn't far away. Twenty miles, maybe. It's still Cobb County, which is the county I've lived in since 1995—just shy of twenty successive years split between the towns of Kennesaw, Acworth, and Smyrna.

So one might think, given all the time I've been around here—even without considering those twenty years, just focusing on the past four—that I would feel connected to this place. I don't. I want to, but I really don't. Given that connection to place means so much to me—Wendell Berry's influence on me has been profound, if that gives you some sense of what I'm talking about—and that I've tried and am still trying to find connection in this place, the disconnect I've felt and continue to feel here is itself a kind of loss. There are some things I'm trying to do to make that connection—I'm hoping to help establish a local literary scene, for example, working with a new cultural arts center in town (which I think is a blessing), but that sense of belonging still isn't there. Most of the time I feel like an outsider, a stranger, even though this is a place that I know and love. I guess this is especially true during political campaign seasons or in times of national crisis. This place is very pro-gun, for example, and in the wake of Sandy Hook, some people from around here didn't hesitate to let everybody know it. It was very upsetting. But of course my privilege plays a part here, too: At the end of the day, it's easy for me to fade into the background, into the crowd.

I'm glad you say that *Everything Turns Away* managed to transcend mourning and sadness, though, because sadness drove this book to completion in more ways than I probably know. I've never really talked about this publicly or even in the context of my writing, but for the past three or so years, I've been estranged from my mother and stepfather—and my little brother, as a result. They live about five minutes down the road, and they were the ones I lived with when I was going to high school here. It's been a long time coming, I suppose, as these things don't generally come out of nowhere. But I've felt incredibly sad and burdened over the past couple years, which is roughly the timeframe in which I wrote most of the poems that made it into *Everything Turns Away*.

I suppose this sadness just made the sense of loss and the recognition of impending loss that Bass was talking about more acute in the context of the place from which these poems emerged.

Take the poem "Gulf Fritillaries, Allatoona Creek," which to me is a key poem in *Everything Turns Away*, functioning as a sort of bridge: It invokes the violent history of this place, from the Trail of Tears to slavery and the Civil War, as well as the current tendency toward suburbanization and homogenization, and contains certain images that reflect this place's pathos—Confederate flags (which, incidentally, seem to have proliferated in the wake of what happened in Charleston), church signs talking about the devil and hell, NRA decals, and so on.

Yet, as Hopkins wrote, there still "lives the dearest freshness deep down things," and being awake to these things (or maybe it's better to say being awakened by them)—whether butterflies on coyote shit or children splashing around in some insignificant creek—helped prevent this pervading sense of loss from turning into morbidity over the course of writing this book. There's a ring of hope to it, too.

[*Poecology*] I recently read an article in *The Atlantic* titled "The Poem That Made Sherman Alexie Want to 'Drop Everything and Be a Poet.'" Do you have a poem like that? If so, how do you see the inspiration of that poem appearing in your current work?

[CM] Thanks for leading me to that article—it's really great, and I'm sure I'll keep returning to it. Funny thing, synchronous thing, is that Sherman Alexie links what he's saying to some of the themes that have emerged in our interview here—when he writes, for example, "So you can see the broader applicability: *I'm in the suburb of my mind.*"

I guess the poem I'd select would be any of a handful from *Leaves of Grass*—"Song of Myself" if I had to choose. In 2005, at twenty-two, I took a semester off college, distanced myself for the first time ever from a toxic situation at home, and went for a 500-mile walk on the Appalachian Trail, from Damascus, Virginia to Harper's Ferry, West Virginia. I'd been seriously reading Thoreau and Martin Luther King, Jr. for about a year or so up to that point, and I finished *Walden* not long at all before I left. I took *Walden* on the hike with me to read again, and also read *Narrative of the Life of Frederick Douglass* early in the hike. I eventually sent those home so I could carry *The Autobiography of Malcolm X* and *Leaves of Grass.* When I got home, I started reading Annie Dillard, Wendell Berry, Thomas Merton, Janisse Ray. All these books and writers, and a few others, were the ones who shook me awake and got me to take my voice and my writing seriously.

And old R.E.M. Always old R.E.M. Without their music as part of my subconscious since I was about twelve, I don't think any of the books I just mentioned would've hit me the way they did at twenty-two.

But I guess Walt Whitman is the main one who got me thinking seriously about poetry. Lines like these from "Song of Myself" come to mind:

The sickness of one of my folks or of myself, or ill-doing or loss or
    lack of money, or depressions or exaltations,

141

Battles, the horrors of fratricidal war, the fever of doubtful news, the
    fitful events;
These come to me days and nights and go from me again,
But they are not the Me myself.

It was at the very end of my hike that I really connected to those lines and so much else from that poem. I'd gotten [some bad news from home], so I was worried about
going back but also knew that I needed to go back. Even
out there on the Trail, I was "in the suburb of my mind,"
and Whitman, maybe even more than Thoreau, helped me
navigate that with words like these:

I have said that the soul is not more than the body,
And I have said that the body is not more than the soul,
And nothing, not God, is greater to one than one's self is,
And whoever walks a furlong without sympathy walks to his
    own funeral drest in his shroud,
And I or you pocketless of a dime may purchase the pick of
    the earth,
And to glance with an eye or show a bean in its pod confounds
    the learning of all times,
And there is no trade or employment but the young man fol-
    lowing it may become a hero,
And there is no object so soft but it makes a hub for the
    wheel'd universe,
And I say to any man or woman, Let your soul stand cool and
    composed before a million universes.
And I say to mankind, Be not curious about God,
For I who am curious about each am not curious about God.
(No array of terms can say how much I am at peace about God
    and about death.)
I hear and behold God in every object, yet understand God
    not in the least,

Nor do I understand who there can be more wonderful than
    myself.
Why should I wish to see God better than this day?
I see something of God each hour of the twenty-four, and
    each moment then,
In the faces of men and women I see God, and in my own face
    in the glass,
I find letters from God dropt in the street, and every one is
    sign'd by God's name,
And I leave them where they are, for I know that wheresoe'er
    I go
Others will punctually come for ever and ever.

That will wake you up in the morning—or in my case, before falling asleep on the porch of a hostel outside of Harper's Ferry, looking out at the stars, on one of my last nights on the AT, worrying about things.

As to how it inspires my current work, I guess I'm just trying to show some of those letters I've found dropped in the street by God, or whatever you call God, whatever I call God—to show that, like Whitman said, those letters keep on coming, and they'll keep coming forever, wherever I go, wherever we go. R.E.M.'s "These Days" has kind of the same message: "All the people gather, fly to carry each his burden / We are young despite the years / We are concern, we are hope despite the times / All of a sudden these days, happy throngs take this joy / Wherever, wherever you go."

This is essentially what informs my poetry. If I ever talk about violence, about desecration, about irreverence, it's because I think it's best that we hold and read and live by these dropped letters rather than rip them up and burn them, or just toss them aside because we assume we'll never understand them. And I'm talking to myself here more than anyone.

If I've ever been able to get just one word of any of those letters into any of my poems, into anything I write, it's a miracle. But the real miracle, the real work that goes well beyond anything I or anyone else writes, is realizing that we are those letters, too, and to go forward in that knowledge. It's a difficult knowledge to hold close, but I don't think anything is more lovely or essential.

Notes

Book epigraphs: The passage from the Gospel of John is a slightly adapted version of John 1:4 – 5 using the Humble American/American Koine translation as presented in the American Folk Gospel (Coiny Publishing, 1999). The passage from the Gospel of Mary is my rendering of Karen L. King's translation as presented in *The Gospel of Mary of Magdala: Jesus and the First Woman Apostle* (Santa Rosa: Polebridge Press, 2003).

Preface epigraph: This is my adaptation based on consulting and combining multiple translations of Job 41, as well as other instances where Leviathan is mentioned in the Old Testament.

Phos Hilaron: "The rain I am in...": Thomas Merton, "Rain and the Rhinoceros." *Raids on the Unspeakable* (New York: New Directions, 1964).

Formed by Water: First epigraph: Mary Oliver, "Going to Walden." *New and Selected Poems: Volume One* (Boston: Beacon Press, 1992). | "A little band of dedicated Thoreauvians...": E.B. White, "A Slight Sound at Evening." *Essays of E.B. White* (New York: Harper Colophon, 1979).

Original Sound: "In the massed crowd": Merton, "The Time of the End is the Time of No Room." *Raids on the Unspeakable.* | "We are human": Merton, *Conjectures of a Guilty Bystander* (New York: Image Books, 1968). | "Shoulder your duds": Walt Whitman, "Song of Myself." |

"here not even the surface had been scarred": Henry David Thoreau, "Ktaadn." *The Maine Woods.*

Treasure This Ecstasy: "Love to throw yourself on the earth" through "Treasure this ecstasy": Fyodor Dostoevsky, *The Brothers Karamazov*, Book VI: "The Russian Monk," Ch. 2, "Conversations and Exhortations of Father Zossima." | I once wrote an essay: The essay in question was an early draft of what is now "Original Sound." The scene in question was the drive to the hospital.

Assaying a Garden: "The completely irreligious mind": Merton, *Conjectures of a Guilty Bystander.*

Walking Around Shining: "in the center of the shopping district": Merton, *Conjectures of a Guilty Bystander.*

Part II epigraph: Merton, *Thoughts in Solitude* (New York: Farrar, Straus, and Giroux, 1958).

"Meditation on a Little Boy Touching His Face": Merton, *The Seven Storey Mountain* (New York: Harcourt Brace and Company, 1948).

Reckoning These Ruins: "there is an entire system of injustice": Roxane Gay, "On the Death of Sandra Bland and Our Vulnerable Bodies." *New York Times*, July 2015. Online. | "...it's clear that we as an American society have forgotten": Shannon M. Houston, "No Mourning, No Peace: Sam Dubose, Sandra Bland, and Why Black Lives Don't Matter (Yet)." *Salon*, July 2015. Online.

Of War and the Red-Tailed Hawk: "It is enough to make the whole world start": Quoted in Earl Hess, *Kennesaw Mountain: Sherman, Johnston, and the Atlanta Campaign* (Chapel Hill: University of North Carolina Press, 2003).

Thoreau's Gift: In his early work: All quotes in this paragraph are from *A Week on the Concord and Merrimack Rivers*. | "The murderous din" through "Let me seek": Merton, *Thoughts in Solitude*. | "I love Henry": Quoted in Ralph Waldo Emerson, "Thoreau." | At my university: Now *alma mater*.

The Wren Whistling in the Garden: "You cannot be a man of faith": Merton, *New Seeds of Contemplation* (New York: New Directions, 1962). | "Bible says gays should be stoned." Teresa Masterson, "Man, 70, Stoned to Death for Being Gay" (*NBC Philadelphia*, March 18, 2011; accessed online July 1, 2011). Note: In light of current events centered on homophobia, transphobia, and continued discrimination against the LGBTQ community—take the passage and support of North Carolina's HB2, for example—this section needs expansion, which I would do if such expansion wouldn't also disrupt the general timeframe against which these fragments are set. But suffice it to say in these notes that the problem cannot be reduced to any single troubling event or act of violence. For example, whether or not most Christians would condone actually killing or physically hurting someone for being gay, it is a question that far too many Christians take seriously. This, of course, was the subject of a recent rant, in November 2015, by pastor Kevin Swanson at the National Religious Liberties Conference before introducing three Republican presidential candidates, including Ted Cruz. None of the candidates seemed too concerned that Swanson had just pondered aloud for a prolonged time about whether or not the government should execute gay people. Swanson reached the conclusion that the government need not enact such a policy, at least not yet, because God would be settling the matter with eternal hellfire—and on this note, he is far from being alone. For more, see Katherine Stewart, "Ted Cruz and the Anti-Gay Pastor," *New York Times*, November 2015. | "I wish, O Son of the living God": Quoted in Christopher Bamford and William Parker Marsh, eds., *Celtic Christianity: Ecology and Holiness* (Great Barrington: Lindisfarne Press, 1987). | "The first man who whistled": Wendell Berry, "The First." *Given* (Shoemaker and Hoard, 2006). |

Christ of the Burnt Men: "know the Christ of the burnt men": Merton, *The Seven Storey Mountain.* | "all the trees of the wood": Psalm 96:12, KJV | "mountains and hills": Isaiah 55:12, KJV | "The test of observance of Christ's teachings": Quoted in Philip Yancey, *Soul Survivor: How Thirteen Unlikely Mentors Helped My Faith Survive the Church* (New York: Galilee, 2003).

Rooted in Her Body: "lovely in limbs": Gerard Manley Hopkins, "As kingfishers catch fire."

Appendix: Go to the Ground: "I think of the poet Camille Dungy": Natasha Trethewey with William Wright, "Speak Against the Silences: An Interview with Natasha Trethewey." *Atlanta Review*, October 2013.

Acknowledgments

Thanks to Cristina Martin, Nicole Knox, Molly Dickinson, and Rachel Trignano of *Loose Change*, Bobbi Buchanan of *New Southerner*, Thomas Rain Crowe of New Native Press, Will Wright of *The Southern Poetry Anthology* (among other projects), and Cheryl Stiles of La Vita Poetica Press for believing in my work at such an early stage. Your friendship and encouragement have meant a great deal. Thanks to Tony Grooms, David King, Kathleen Brewin Lewis, Janisse Ray, and Erik Reece for your writing, your guidance, your friendship, and your support. Thanks to Paul Bodamer, Darren Crovitz, Faith Wallace, and Sara Worley for your teaching years ago and helping me find the spark.

Thanks to all associated with the publications in which parts of this book first appeared, sometimes in different form: *Adventum*, *The Good Men Project*, *LETTERS: A Journal of Yale Divinity School and Institute of Sacred Music*, *Loose Change Magazine*, *Menacing Hedge*, *New Southerner*, *Old Red Kimono*, *Parable Press*, *Poecology*, *Revolution House*, *Sanctuary*, *Still: The Journal*, and *Town Creek Poetry*. A special thanks here to editors Kristi Moos, Charlie Bondhus, Win Bassett, Jason Howard and Marianne Worthington.

A reading of an early version of "Original Sound," recorded at *lostintheletters* in Atlanta, aired on Crescent Hill Radio's *Keep Hearing Voices* (with thanks to Scott Daughtridge and Marie Direction). "Phos Hilaron" was reprinted in *The Best of Loose Change*. "My Children Pile Sticks on a Headstone" was first published as a limited-edition broadside, along with a poem by David King, by

Occasional Snakes Press. "The Wish to Sing with Primitive Baptists" and "At the Etowah Mounds" appeared in the chapbook *Everything Turns Away* (La Vita Poetica Press, 2014). "My Daughter Laughs in Her Sleep" won the 2014 Georgia Scarbrough Award for Poetry, presented by the Mountain Heritage Literary Festival at Lincoln Memorial University, selected by Aaron Smith.

Thanks to everyone I've met through literary communities from Atlanta to Appalachia and beyond. Thanks to everyone at Wildbranch and *Orion* for the early inspiration. Thanks to everyone at One For Ten for the work you do in fighting injustice, and for the privilege of working alongside you for a time. Thanks to everyone at the Acworth Cultural Arts Center. Thanks to everyone who's been part of *Flycatcher*. Thanks to my students at the Appalachian Young Writers Workshop and Georgia Highlands College, alongside whom I wrote some of the newer parts of this book.

The Appalachian Young Writers Workshop has been like a family to me over these last three summers. To Darnell Arnoult, Jesse Graves, Belinda Smith, Lacey Cook, Mike D., Langston Wilkins, Robert Gipe, Susan Gregg Gilmore, Wendy Dinwiddie, Joseph Ellison, Brittany Skidmore, and Brittany Gray: Thank you. I'm honored to be part of what you're doing. Thanks also to friends, professors, colleagues, and students at Kennesaw State. A special thanks to professors and fellow alums of KSU MAPW—Terri Brennen, Laura Dabundo, Jim Elledge, Beth Giddens, Todd Harper, Imani Marshall-Stephen, Linda Niemann, Karen Pickell, Laurence Stacey, Precious Williams, Ralph Wilson, and so many others—for making my time in the program as special as it was.

Thanks to Rosemary Royston, Denton Loving, Craig McDonald, and Jordan Thrasher. I appreciate y'all. Thanks to everyone not already named who has helped me along the writing path in some way, whether as friends, colleagues, coworkers, teachers, readers, editors, publishers, reading organizers, inspirations, or some combination of these. To everyone who has shaped me and been there for me outside of a literary capacity, you have my gratitude.

To Marc Jolley, Mary Beth Kosowski, Marsha Lutrell, and everyone at Mercer University Press, thank you for all you've done for me and this book.

I am incredibly humbled that this book has been recognized with an award named for Reverend Will Campbell, and I only hope it will honor his legacy.

Thanks to Jennifer Martin and Sarah Martin, my sisters and heroes, for always being there for me and being here still. I love you both.

This book is dedicated to Deana, Cannon, and Opal. I hope what love and thankfulness I have for you, and what abiding joy I have because of you, will come through in this book, and that what I cannot express in this book will come through in a lifetime. I wouldn't be a thing without you. You have my heart and you are my heart.

About the Author

2015 Will D. Campbell Award winner Christopher Martin lives with his family in northwest Georgia, between the Allatoona Range and Kennesaw Mountain. Martin is author of three poetry chapbooks, and his essays and poems have appeared in publications across the country, including American Public Media's *On Being* and *Shambhala Sun*. The founding editor of *Flycatcher*, a contributing editor at *New Southerner*, and erstwhile stay-at-home parent, Martin teaches English at Kennesaw State University and creative nonfiction at the Appalachian Young Writers Workshop. *This Gladdening Light* is Martin's nonfiction book debut, and his full-length debut of any genre. You can find him online at www.christopher-martin.net.

Index